PRO**ACTIVE**
Classroom
Management
K–8

PRO**ACTIVE** **Classroom Management K–8**

A PRACTICAL GUIDE TO EMPOWER STUDENTS AND TEACHERS

LOUIS G. **DENTI**

CORWIN
A SAGE Company

CORWIN
A SAGE Company

FOR INFORMATION:

Corwin
A SAGE Company
2455 Teller Road
Thousand Oaks, California 91320
(800) 233-9936
Fax: (800) 417-2466
www.corwin.com

SAGE Publications Ltd.
1 Oliver's Yard
55 City Road
London EC1Y 1SP
United Kingdom

SAGE Publications India Pvt. Ltd.
B 1/I 1 Mohan Cooperative Industrial Area
Mathura Road, New Delhi 110 044
India

SAGE Publications Asia-Pacific Pte. Ltd.
33 Pekin Street #02-01
Far East Square
Singapore 048763

Acquisitions Editor: Jessica Allan
Associate Editor: Allison Scott
Editorial Assistant: Lisa Whitney
Production Editor: Amy Schroller
Copy Editor: Janet Ford
Typesetter: C&M Digitals (P) Ltd.
Proofreader: Jeff Bryant
Indexer: Sheila Bodell
Cover Designer: Karine Hovsepian
Permissions Editor: Karen Ehrmann

Printed in the United States of America

Library of Congress Cataloging-in-Publication Data

Denti, Lou

Proactive classroom management, K-8 : a practical guide to empower students and teachers / Louis G. Denti.

p. cm.
Includes bibliographical references and index.

ISBN 978-1-4522-0389-8 (pbk.)

1. Classroom management—United States.
2. Behavior modification—United States.
3. School discipline—United States. I. Title.

LB3013.D468 2012
371.102′4—dc23   2011043025

This book is printed on acid-free paper

SUSTAINABLE FORESTRY INITIATIVE

Certified Chain of Custody
Promoting Sustainable Forestry
www.sfiprogram.org
SFI-01268

SFI label applies to text stock

12 13 14 15 16 10 9 8 7 6 5 4 3 2 1

Contents

PART II: ACTIVITIES TO PROMOTE POSITIVE CLASSROOM AND STUDENT BEHAVIOR   **75**

Acknowledgments

I personally would like to thank all the teachers who work so diligently to support students, with and without challenges, in our public schools. Most people can recall a teacher who helped guide them on the path to success. This book is written for hard-working teachers/educators everywhere who toil day in and day out in our schools. I would also like to thank Kevin Feldman for some of his good thoughts found in the Teacher Discipline Checklist, Diana Browning Wright for her suggestions regarding class meetings, Anita Archer whose ideas in some form or fashion are sprinkled throughout the book, and my friend John Abramson for his clever metaphors, for example, "the yellow light always goes off before the red light" signaling teachers to be proactive instead of reactive. My heartfelt thanks go to Jessica Allan from Corwin for believing that this book can help teachers now and in the future.

Many teachers helped develop these activities, and I would like to take this opportunity to thank them all:

Marjorie Addison	JoAnn Diel	Linda Grand
Brendan Baer	Mary H. Dominquez	Marc Guastavino
Lynn Beebe	David Eberwein	Cindy Hammel
Pat Benstein	Folse Eberwein	Kevin Hendrix
Ethan Bernstein	Kaye Edwards	Cheryl Hill
Leah Boyd	Esther Erman	Kathy Holcomb
Cindy Broersma	Janice Finch	Terry Jacobs
Michele Burruss	Sandy Frame	Kim Jarman
Malia Cahalan	Tricia Gallagher-Geurtsen	Ann Jones
Wendy Cargile	Melissa Gamino	Charity Joy
Rick Cole	Nancy Goldsmith	Freya Kidner
Paige Crowder	Elena Goldstein	Carol Marshall

(Continued)

(Continued)

Suzy Morganstern

Robert Moss

Lisa Newman

Lesa Nieri

Terry O'Conner

Karen W. Officer

Kellene O'Neill-Hinckley

Joan Post

Elizabeth Rible

Judy Sakasegawa

Kathy Schleiff

Roberta Schultze

Michele Shepherd

Sharon L. Smith

Lucetta Swift

Quentin Tagara

Geoffrey E. Thompson

Chau Tran

Shelly Viramontez

Sarah Warren

Lihuei Wei

Georgina Wong

Roberta Wright

About the Author

Dr. Louis G. Denti, a former special educator and administrator, is currently the Lawton Love Distinguished Professor of Special Education at California State University, Monterey Bay. His research focuses on student behavior, special education, inclusion, and literacy.

Lou has dedicated his life to helping those who struggle to learn. Educators across the country have benefited from his research, publications, and presentations. In 2009, he delivered the keynote address at the annual meeting of the Ohio School Speech Pathology and Educational Audiology Consortium and received the organization's Annie Glenn National Leadership Award. The award is named for Annie Glenn, wife of former astronaut and Senator John Glenn, and an adjunct professor in the Department of Speech and Hearing Science at Ohio State University.

Introduction

This book began as a class project in a behavior management course at San Jose State University for special education teachers. The teachers were asked to create or adapt an activity that they used to help with classroom management. The conditions for the assignment were fairly basic: make certain the activity is something you or any teacher can implement, that it is easy to understand, and that the consequences, if applied, are reasonable and respectful of students. A template was developed to aid the students in writing up their activity. The activity was peer reviewed and then given the stamp of approval by the instructor. What seemed like an easy activity proved to be quite challenging for the teachers/students. They often commented that although they used a particular behavior method almost daily, it was difficult to explain it for other teachers to use. Using fewer words to convey the essence of the selected behavior activity without sacrificing intent or content was the greatest challenge. The activities listed in Part II have been through several iterations with much editing on the author's part. The activities then went through another layer of scrutinization and editing from a seasoned special educator, Pam Eiriksson.

By no means are these activities the last word regarding classroom management. They are meant to pique an educator's interest with the hope that one of the activities will be implemented or adapted. Along those lines, it is the author's intent that educators will share the book and photocopy activities for other educators or parents to use.

We would all love to have the perfect, well-behaved classroom…but does it really exist? There are days when you as the teacher are not feeling in top shape and there are days when individuals in the class are out of sorts too. I have found it comforting to know that I have a behavioral system in place that helps to see me through those days when I don't feel up to dealing with misbehavior. You probably have students in your class that despite your earnest efforts, high expectations, respect, and clear requirements still haven't quite tied in with the class. They are students that need more support to function successfully in class. The following activities are great examples and ways to encourage positive individual and whole-class behavior. Pick the activities that are right for you and your class and try them out. Modify them to fit your style, use them as a base to create your own, or use them as is. Enjoy this great resource!

—Pamela Eiriksson
Special Education Teacher of 10+ years
Boulder Creek Elementary

BOOK ORGANIZATION

The book is divided into two parts. Part I titled *Proactive Teaching and Empowering Students* provides teachers with general classroom operating principles for establishing and maintaining classroom control. It goes beyond the mechanics of classroom management by offering time-tested ideas and strategies to enhance self-esteem in students. Part I creates the context for many of the activities suggested in Part II. The ideas in the first section encourage teachers to be proactive and students to take responsibility for their actions and feelings. Vignettes highlight some of the concepts included in this section by grounding the ideas in scenarios that teachers encounter daily. Ways to deal with overactive students or students identified with attention deficit disorder (ADD) are also covered in this section.

Chapter 6 details *Nine Features for Effective Classroom Management and Student Empowerment* and is aimed at helping teachers with day-to-day classroom management. This chapter appeals to teacher sensibilities by providing practical ideas and techniques to empower both students and teachers. For example, Feature 2 in this chapter helps teachers with a simple data collection process, and Feature 6 describes how classroom meetings empower students to be more cognizant of their behavior in order to take responsibility for their actions.

Part II lists *Activities to Promote Positive Classroom and Student Behavior* and is chock full of teacher-friendly activities to promote an enhanced classroom environment. The activities are separated into five categories from lower elementary through junior high school. The following checklist gives the teacher a snapshot of activities allowing them to choose any one, or several, activities that fit their individual style. You will notice activities that you have seen in use at your school or variations of familiar activities and, of course, some new ones to pique your interest.

QUICK GLANCE AT PART II: ACTIVITIES TO ENCOURAGE POSITIVE BEHAVIOR

Activity	Grades K–2	Grades 3–5	Grades K–8	Grades 6–8
"2:45 p.m.–3:00 p.m." Store	X	X	X	
Accomplishment Journal	X	X	X	X
Achievement Chart				X
Achieving the Spirit of Academic Excellence				X
Adventures of "Regie"	X	X	X	
All Smiles	X	X	X	
Assignment Jar				X
Author/Scientist Chair		X		

Activity	Grades K–2	Grades 3–5	Grades K–8	Grades 6–8
Beebe's Bucks				X
Boost for Homework	X	X	X	
Brain Food	X	X	X	
Bravo Point System	X	X	X	
Campus Stewards	X	X	X	X
Caught Being Good	X	X	X	
CEO's				X
Chance Tickets	X	X	X	
Characters	X	X	X	
Choose a Card	X	X	X	
Classroom Store	X	X	X	X
Colored Cards	X	X	X	
Earn the Activity of Your Choice	X			
Fun Friday Choices	X	X	X	
Giving Positives	X	X	X	X
Good Group Award	X	X	X	
Group Points		X		
Homework Pass	X	X	X	X
Individual Rewards	X	X	X	X
Kill the Curiosity				X
Kind and Caring Tickets	X	X	X	
Large Group Rhythm	X			
Large Group Singing	X			
Lender Binder		X		X
Long Journey Home	X	X	X	
Look at Me				X
Lunch With Teacher	X	X	X	
Marbles in a Jar	X	X	X	
Mr. Steven's Bucks	X	X	X	
Name in the Heart Box	X	X	X	
Number Club	X	X	X	
Olympics				X
Pass Challenge				X
Pay Well to Those Who Play Well	X	X	X	
Pizza Challenge		X		X
Popsicle Sticks	X			
Privilege Auction	X	X	X	X

(Continued)

(Continued)

Activity	Grades K–2	Grades 3–5	Grades K–8	Grades 6–8
Question Box	X	X	X	X
Red Light–Green Light	X	X	X	
Resource Points				X
Self Talk	X	X	X	X
Sharing the News	X	X	X	
Sharing Time	X			
Show 'n' Tell	X			
Smiley Faces	X			
Soapbox				X
Stamp Your Way to Good Behavior	X	X	X	
Star of the Week	X	X	X	X
Star Jar	X	X	X	
Stars, "Dollars," and *La Tiendita*	X	X	X	
Stickers for All Seasons	X			
Stickers on Paper	X	X	X	
Stoplight	X	X	X	
Surprise Money				X
Table of the Week	X	X	X	X
"Teacher" Dollars		X		
Teacher's Shop	X			
Team Leaders	X	X	X	
Thank You Cards	X	X	X	X
Thermometer	X	X	X	
Thumb Prints	X	X	X	
Tickets	X	X	X	
Unit Log/"Table of Contents"		X		
VIP Passes				X
Wall Map		X		
Watch Me Grow	X	X	X	
Weekly Grid		X		
Without a Raffle	X	X	X	
Yellow/Blue Sheet Rewards	X	X	X	X

PART I

Proactive Teaching and Empowering Students

It's far more important to be the right kind
of teacher than it is to be the right kind of student.

—Denti

Consider this guiding statement or thought as you progress through the book. Oftentimes when there are management challenges in your classroom, it is easy to blame the student, his or her family, or the community where the student comes from, rather than analyze what you as a teacher might be doing to contribute to some of the issues. Don't get me wrong, some children, for whatever the reason, can be difficult and get on your proverbial nerves. However, you should remember that those students comprise only a small number compared to the students who love school and enjoy being in your class. I know that often a teacher's grey hairs can be caused by the behavior problems of a few. Interestingly, most teachers comment on the few students who cause problems rather than commenting on the students who comply and progress through the curriculum taking advantage of good instruction and timely encouragement. In workshops I conduct, I use the example of a dream about a giant multi-ton barge, shrouded in darkness and fog, coming to you the classroom teacher. The barge captain, positioned stoically on the bow, yells out through a megaphone, "What kids would you like to get rid of so you can have a great year?" You can't believe it and are so thankful that the captain has come your way. You immediately respond, "How about these 10 students?" The barge captain obliges and the next morning you walk into class and all of the 10 students who exhibited minor to major behavior problems (some just wouldn't put their name on the right hand corner of the page even though you reminded them time and time again) are *gone*! The next week goes by and then you have the same reoccurring dream and the barge captain once again asks, "Want to get rid of a few more students?" Your reply is a resounding "Yes!" So you get rid of about 5 more students. The barge captain keeps showing up in your dream until you are down to 1 student and you yell out, "Now I can finally teach!" You are so relieved. You can now work one on one, watching the student progress in front of your very eyes, instead of hoping that you get through to most of your students or that they will behave and learn what is expected from a particular grade-level curriculum.

I know that you may find this exaggerated example funny, but in humor there is always a grain of truth. The truth is that there are days that all of us would like to be able to ship kids out that don't want to learn or cause headaches. Maybe you'd like to order up that imaginary barge to come take your troublemakers away to another classroom, another school, or another state. Unfortunately, the kids with problems just keep coming and that's the reason for this book. There are no barges to take kids away. You can identify children for special education or have them attend a specialized class for math or English, but invariably you, the general education teacher, are responsible for the bulk of their education. And this is no easy task. Both this chapter and this book offer no panaceas. They do offer ways to improve your teaching and classroom management skills, enhance your knowledge base, and help you maintain a positive attitude so you can be proactive.

Proactive teaching simply means that a teacher anticipates what will happen and when, rather than waiting for something to occur and then reacting, oftentimes inappropriately. It requires tremendous preparation and vigilance to head problems off before they escalate into full-blown meltdowns, confrontations, or withdrawals. Proactive teachers do not give up or give in. Instead of imagining a barge captain coming to take kids away, they see themselves as responsible for creating a positive, learning environment for all students. The chapters in Part I define proactive teaching and student empowerment in more depth, focusing on ways that teachers can take and maintain control in their classrooms.

1

Empowering Students Through Proactive Teaching

Several years ago, I heard about a teacher who lined her students up in order from beginning to end in a very inequitable manner. The beginning of the line had students who could pay for their lunch, second in line were students who could partially pay, and the back or end of the line were students who received free lunch. The students at the end of the line would slink to the back of the line with their eyes peeled to the floor, while the students who could pay for their lunch would strut confidently to the front of the line. The students in the middle wanted to be associated with the students at the front of the line and disregarded the students at the back of the line. The teacher had set up a situation where students at the back of the line were disempowered and felt like second-class citizens. The students in the front of the line felt a sense of entitlement; the students in the middle aligned themselves with what could be perceived as the high-status position; while the students in the back felt inferior or unequal. This teacher had knowingly set up a situation wherein students were treated with disrespect and disdain. One can only surmise the effect on these students during their tenure in the class and in later years to come. Make no mistake, teachers have tremendous power and authority to create an environment where students feel cared for, needed, and empowered. They can also do the opposite as is evident in this example. I trust that when reading this story you were as bothered as I was at this teacher's actions and behavior toward her students. So let's turn our attention to the ways teachers can be proactive and empower students to be their best.

Being proactive entails a conscientious effort on the part of teachers to provide a classroom environment that allows students to be themselves, take risks, learn from mistakes, and understand how to take responsibility for their actions and feelings. A proactive teacher acts in advance to deal with expected difficulty. He or she controls the expected occurrence causing something to happen rather than reacting after something has happened. A proactive teacher maintains high standards, sets limits, applies consequences responsibly and most importantly creates a learning environment that is fun and encouraging. You never hear students talk about how much science or math they learned in a class. They do always talk about a teacher they liked or disliked. And without a doubt, the teacher who creates a caring and trusting atmosphere with clearly defined limits always garners praise from students. When teachers react inconsistently to student behavioral challenges or lay in wait to catch a student for misbehaving, students begin to mistrust their teacher. Then either the child avoids the teacher or does something negative to get the teacher's attention. For every negative action by the teacher there is an equal and opposite negative action by the student—*good ole Newton's Law*. Likewise, for every positive action students respond accordingly. A proactive teacher values students, anticipates problems, and sets up a learning environment that captivates student interest and attention. The teacher creates the context for student empowerment.

Empowerment can best be defined as providing a child or student with a sense of confidence, capability, competence, and self-esteem to meet life's challenges. Although the word empowerment has been overused and sometimes misused, it still holds tremendous value and allows individuals to feel that they are important and can make a difference in the world. In education, *empowering* is a process that takes time and commitment on a teacher's part to ensure that children and youth develop a positive self-image, have decision-making power, and most importantly, have a range of options from which to make healthy, informed choices. Adults act as important role models empowering children and youth with the necessary social and learning tools to deal with life's many ups and downs. They proactively "model the way," laying the foundation for lifelong learning. The best teachers gently nudge children along the path to success. They often empower a child to do more than they ever believed possible. However for students to reach their potential, teachers must apply limits and consequences in order to teach positive behavior. These life lessons help children to become self-reliant and capable adults. A classroom wherein the teacher encourages positive student and classroom behavior provides the opportunity for beneficial learning inside and outside the classroom.

RECOGNITION AND ENCOURAGEMENT

Student empowerment starts with recognition and encouragement from proactive educators. When teachers recognize student achievement and effort in a clear, consistent manner, students feel more capable and competent and are, in turn, more willing to learn. When teachers encourage students to be their best, they will live up to the teacher's expectations, time and time again. Personalizing recognition by giving students either a tangible award (a sticker, a tally mark, a homework pass) or a non-tangible award (verbal compliment, a high five) increases a student's perseverance to task and increases their self esteem. In their book *Classroom Instruction That Works*, Marzano, Pickering and Pollack identify a number of essential strategies backed by research that impact academic performance. One of the vital strategies happens to be reinforcing effort and providing recognition. It could be implied that a teacher's statements of "good job," or "way to go," or "good boy, good girl" indicate the teacher's satisfaction with a student or child's task performance. Although one could walk into any class in the country and hear teachers delivering countless similar statements, Marzano and his coauthors' research does not endorse such an approach. Their research reinforces the view that recognition should be tied to a standard of achievement, a standard that the student values (good grades), or that the teacher values (completes assignments on time). A *good girl or good boy* helps to make a child feel worthy; however, it does not specifically give him or her feedback on what is done well. *Recognition* must be clearly defined, directed, and measurable so that the student understands exactly what he or she is doing well. Designing weekly goals with students where they log in their efforts and achievements and then reflect on them with a peer or the teacher can be most empowering. Many of the activities found in Part I of this book provide a foundation for recognizing and honoring students for their achievements and for taking responsibility for their actions.

On the other hand, *encouragement* can be a bit tricky. Unlike recognition, it does not have to be tied to a specific achievement standard or award, but must be ongoing, supportive, clear, and definitely make the student feel empowered and capable. The adage "one to grow on and ten to glow on" appears to be more important nowadays than ever before. Students need corrective feedback (one to grow on) given in a kind and supportive manner and they need an "obnoxious" amount of encouragement (ten to glow on) to continue to learn from the task at hand. When teachers encourage students to be their best, they send a clear and convincing message that they care deeply for them and kids feel and know when encouragement is genuine. Phrases such as "I really like the way you solved that problem, keep up the good work," or "Can you tell me how you both figured that out? The two of you are quite brilliant, don't you both agree?" send such a powerful and empowering message to students that the shine bouncing off of their smiles can light up the classroom. Purposeful and continuous encouragement is the mark of a proactive teacher and, in turn, the mark of secure agile students. The following vignettes point out the stark differences between a teacher who builds an encouraging environment that students trust versus a teacher who betrays the trust in students thus creating a dispiriting climate.

Mrs. Yenez always has something nice to say about her sixth-grade students. She posts statements throughout her room such as, *You are EXTRAordinary, You are IMPORTANT, and You are SOMEBODY*. Not only does Mrs. Yenez dot her room with encouraging words, she backs it up with very specific comments related to students on task behavior. For instance, when Joshua completed his assignment before others, she was quick to acknowledge him. She then had him help another student who found the activity difficult. Students in Mrs. Yenez's classroom feel safe, welcomed, and acknowledged for not only being a good student but for being a good person as well.

In contrast, Ms. Jerrico praises her fourth-grade students continuously with "good boy" and "good girl" statements; however, they are not directly associated with an activity. As a result, in many ways she sounds like a broken record. Students ignore the salutation because she sometimes uses sarcasm indiscriminately and can be harsh with her punishments. Just yesterday, she said, "Good girl Tara" and then lambasted her for having a messy desk with this acerbic comment, "hope your room and house aren't as messy as your desk." The atmosphere in Ms. Jerrico's classroom is one of uncertainty for her students combined with a foreboding sense of underhanded retribution. Students comply with Ms. Jerrico's mercurial demands, yet make snide remarks about her mood swings.

Recognizing and encouraging students, though easy to understand, continues to be difficult for most teachers to do on a consistent basis. Some of the following concepts offer ways to make recognizing and encouraging students a bit easier for teachers.

ESTABLISHING CLEAR GROUND RULES

In Harry and Rosemary Wong's recent book, *The First Days of School: How to Be an Effective Teacher*, they articulate the importance of procedures, clear and realistic expectations, and response strategies when students are out of compliance. On the very first day and the first minute that students enter the classroom, teachers set the tone for either a well-managed or poorly-managed class. Children and adolescents know whether the teacher is in control or not by the way they interact in those first few minutes and hours and in the subsequent weeks ahead. Students are looking for a clear and identified structure with established ground rules for behavior, from requesting to use the bathroom, to lining up, to interacting in small groups, or to using a physical response (like thumbs up) for a request or an answer. Sadly, establishing ground rules though an essential component for a well-run classroom can be difficult to create and reinforce. Teachers tend to employ ground rules when things have gone awry. According to the Wongs, procedures or ground rules distinguish the effective teacher from the noneffective teacher and must be elevated to a high priority and continuously reinforced. Teachers who take the time to develop a set of ground rules, or ways of doing things in the classroom spend less time managing misbehavior and more time teaching. Ground rules can be established in tandem with students, but prior to doing so, it behooves a teacher to have a few well-established ground rules written and thoroughly explained before students weigh in on what they think might be appropriate ground rules. A ground rule that you think might be of utmost importance may not even enter the consciousness of your students. Ground rules that you write down and post above your white board read something like this:

Classroom Ground Rules

- Be ready to learn with your materials on your desk when the bell rings.
- When I am talking, sit up tall and track me with your eyes as I move from place to place.
- Use an *inside* voice—soft, but loud enough to be heard.
- Raise your hand and ask questions only if it is related to what we are studying, for example, "What page are we supposed to be on?" or "I don't understand how to do problem x." Otherwise, *No Hand Raising!*
- Put your hand on your shoulder and tap it lightly if you have a personal request, such as needing to use the bathroom.
- No putdowns (making fun of a student, hurting anyone with mean words) will be tolerated.
- Bullying another student in class will not be tolerated and if it occurs, the bully and the victim will meet with the teacher to discuss appropriate consequences.
- Students who see bullying in the class, on the playground, or anywhere else on campus must notify the teacher or another staff member immediately.

A teacher can suggest that students write ground rules that they think are important for the teacher to abide by and for the class in general to follow. This can be a fun activity but must be closely monitored. Have students think of a few ground rules that help them grow and learn. Ground rules that students might think important for the teacher to follow could read something like this:

Student Ground Rules

- When I talk to my teacher he or she will really listen to me.
- My teacher will not make me feel stupid or embarrass me.
- Our teacher will frequently acknowledge our effort and good work.

Ground rules act as agreements between you and your students and your students and you. You can reinforce a ground rule by simply restating the ground rule and requesting compliance. This form of communication shows students that you value the classroom ground rules, that you will reinforce them, and that you believe students can live up to the established expectations. Ineffective statements such as, "How many times do I have to tell you," or "Do I always have to remind you," are now replaced with pointing to the posted ground rule or signaling students to follow the specific rule. Especially in the first week of school, teachers who take the time to establish and then model the principal rules reduce behavior problems. Well established ground rules help teachers avoid inappropriate and oftentimes immature responses toward students.

In order to ensure that the ground rules will be adhered to by you and your students, follow these very simple yet important guidelines. You will find that a little up-front training on ground rules saves you precious instructional time throughout the year.

1. Develop a few specific ground rules that are clearly defined.

2. Verbally review the ground rules with the students as a whole class.

3. In front of the class, model the ground rules with students by using examples and nonexamples. For instance, for the ground rule *when I am talking, sit up tall and track me with your eyes as I move from place to place*, the teacher can model it the following way. "OK students look at me, now slouch in your chairs (teacher models slouching), now sit up. Do it one more time—slouch and sit up." This is fun for students. "When I indicate track me with your eyes, I am going to go over to the side of the room and I want you to continue to track me. Now I am going over to the other side of the room and I want you to still be tracking me. Good, now when I talk please track me and listen at the same time. Remember to sit up in your chair and listen closely to what I say." The nonexample is slouching, talking to another student, and looking at the ceiling. Model the nonexample, then model the correct way. Reinforce the ground rule by repeating the rule at least two more times. "The ground rule is *when I am talking, sit up tall and track me with your eyes as I move from place to place. Once again the ground rule is *when I am talking, sit up tall and track me with your eyes as I move from place to place.*"

4. Reinforce the ground rules continually with positive statements such as, "I like the way you are following the teacher-talking ground rule. It makes my job a lot easier."

5. Periodically, role-play the ground rules with real examples and non-examples from your class.

6. Tweak, change, add, or rewrite your ground rules as needed.

For your teacher ground rules, revisit them periodically with the students. Ask the students for feedback on how they think you are doing. For student ground rules, poll the class as a whole or ask the students to jot you a note on your progress. You might be surprised at their honesty.

TEACHER COMMITMENT STATEMENTS

I was in a middle school class recently and noticed that the teacher, Mrs. J., had posted a few statements that she would commit to throughout the year. They were simple declarative statements that seemed to fit her demeanor and style of teaching:

I will be on time each and every day unless something unexpected happens.

I will be prepared with a quality lesson.

I will keep learning so I can challenge myself and all of you.

I will respect and honor you and acknowledge you frequently.

I will be available for extra help every day unless I am called to a special meeting of some kind.

I will always care about you.

I asked what was her motivation to write these commitments down for her students and her reply was simple, "They deserve the best *me* and by writing them down it keeps me honest." Writing down a few commitment statements sends a very caring message to your students. It says you are there for them and you can be counted on to act responsibly as an adult. For your class, you might want to consider jotting down a few commitment statements and then discuss your rationale for doing so.

2

Boundaries

Setting clear boundaries for student interaction helps students learn how to communicate effectively. Physical boundaries, such as walls that separate rooms, are easy to visualize and to understand their purpose. Psychological boundaries, like walls that separate rooms, define personal space. When you violate a person's physical or mental state you cross a personal boundary. For students in a classroom, personal boundaries must be addressed and violations handled judiciously and sensitively by the teacher. Some areas of concern for teachers include the use of foul language; shoving and pushing; negative, sarcastic, and stereotypical put-downs; and gossip. Teachers who help students understand that crossing personal boundaries and invading another's personal space are unacceptable help to empower students to take responsibility for their actions. For example, a student might use foul language in front of another student and then browbeat the student for being a *baby* because he or she doesn't use foul language or thinks that using foul language is offensive. This is clearly a psychological boundary violation, where one student harasses another for not using or accepting foul language.

To address boundary violations, teachers can establish ground rules that spell out how students should handle themselves when a violation occurs. It must be stressed that when a student refuses to be bullied, coerced, or cajoled, he or she runs the risk of being ostracized or made fun of by the group. Students who violate boundaries are often perceived to be more powerful by the group and tend to recruit agreement for their actions, thus reinforcing the offending activity. Sometimes violators will threaten to beat up the student if he or she doesn't comply, or call him or her a "tattler" to make him or her feel so uncomfortable that he or she will disregard the established classroom guidelines and not tell the teacher about the incident. As you can see, the violator is often in a more powerful position and armed with the right kind of intimidating language can make any student feel threatened and weaker. This then leads to a cycle of abuse, wherein the abused accepts, goes along with, and sometimes joins in the unacceptable behavior in order to not look or feel foolish in front of other classmates. The only way to stop this cycle is to have boundary ground rules established, monitored, and reinforced. The following boundary ground rules for foul language establish a protocol for both the students and teachers.

Boundary Ground Rules: Foul Language

1. Foul language is not permitted in the classroom or anywhere on campus— No swearing in class or on campus.

2. Foul language used to shock or act cool in front of your friends has no place in our class or at our school.

3. When a student or students use foul language you can politely say, "That makes me feel uncomfortable," and then ask them to stop.

4. Tell the person to find another place to use language like that, away from you.

5. Walk away, and find another group of students to hang out with or return to class.

6. Let the teacher know that foul language was used so your teacher can talk with the violator and, if need be, apply an appropriate consequence.

Without boundary ground rules, teachers tend to impose heavy fines for infractions, counsel students excessively, threaten, or give up and send them to the office. All of the above do not teach acceptable behavior nor do they help the child or student mature and learn to take responsibility for his or her feelings and actions. An empowering classroom has clear standards for student interaction and communication, established ground rules and boundaries, and the teacher monitors and reinforces those standards on a continual basis.

BOUNDARIES FOR OVERACTIVE STUDENTS (ADD AND ADHD)

Every classroom contains students who are overactive. Teachers nowadays face challenges from your ordinary, wiggly, students to students who have significant medical or psychological challenges that cause inattentiveness and hyperactivity. For students who have been medically identified with attention deficit disorder (ADD), or attention deficit hyperactivity disorder (ADHD), teachers must set clear boundaries and establish firm ground rules. Without boundaries and limits, students who exhibit behaviors associated with attention deficit (distractability, inattentiveness, and overactivity) actually become more agitated, and increase their behavioral transgressions. Boundaries with enforced ground rules help students with attention deficit disorder maintain control. In his book, *ADHD and the Nature of Self Control*, Dr. Russell Barkley, a foremost expert on attention deficit disorder exhorts that students with ADD need a clear structure and rules both at school and at home. Structure provides a foundation and an opportunity for students with ADD to manage their behavior responsibly. It must be noted that the structure for a student with ADD in one environment does not necessarily generalize to a different environment. For instance, a classroom teacher may have success with helping a student cope with ADD; however, the PE teacher may not have the same success. In schools there are multiple environments where ADD students interact, so it is important for adults and teachers to understand how to provide these students with the necessary structure along with correct, succinct, verbal instructions to help students regulate their behavior so they can understand what is required to be a successful student. A demanding and authoritarian tone of voice can often increase impulsive, overactive, and inattentive behavior. When adults remain calm, direct, and reinforce stated rules, students with ADD are more apt to comply. Let's take a look a few common scenarios and ways that teachers can deal with students with ADD and ADHD.

Rachel has progressed through the grades at Sunshine Elementary School with a referral to the office sheet longer than an elephant's trunk. She is now in sixth grade and the class and the teacher are baffled at how to help Rachel succeed. She interrupts constantly, blurts out answers, fidgets in her chair, and can't keep her hands to herself. She is unable to complete rudimentary classroom tasks and is easily distracted. Rachel's history of behavioral issues follows her from grade to grade. She has few friends, and those children she does interact with tend to be marginalized by other students in her class and on campus. Her one friend Molly happens to be extremely overweight, and if it weren't for Rachel hanging out with her, she would most likely be a loner. From year to year, the teachers in the lounge tend to discuss Rachel with disdain. However, this year is different. Rachel will be going to the junior high school in a few months and according to her sixth-grade teacher has to *get it together*. Rachel's teacher wants some clear guidelines to help Rachel learn some coping skills that will transfer to junior high school.

So for Rachel, the teacher might follow these guidelines:

- Move Rachel up front to sit right in the center, not to the side.

- Have a student sit next to Rachel to cue her back on task. This student should volunteer to help you with this situation and want to help Rachel. Oftentimes a student who volunteers to help another student becomes a friend outside of class. Make sure Rachel agrees to this arrangement. Try to find a way that this arrangement mutually benefits both students, such as giving each one a free homework pass or another reward that truly means something to them.

- Clarify ground rules and boundaries
  - stay in your seat unless otherwise directed to do so,
  - keep your feet and hands to yourself, track the teacher,
  - thumbs up if you have something the whole class needs to know, like what page we are supposed to be on,

○ tap your shoulders if it is a personal question, such as you need to use the restroom, and

○ ask the student next to you if you need help with a problem or assignment. You must whisper and make it quick. You may only do this one time per period or six times per day.

• Develop an external reward system and make certain that you keep a tally of times you reinforce Rachel (see Part I, Chapter 6, on Data Collection for some ideas). Reinforce positive behavior continually, and then intermittently. Always use Rachel's name when acknowledging her, for example, "Rachel, thank you for using thumbs up when you have an answer." "Rachel, I like the way you are tracking me. That shows you are paying attention." You might put a tally mark on a tally sheet or have Rachel give herself a tally for positive behavior. Make certain that Rachel knows what reward results from her positive behavior.

• Use visual cues. Cut strips of construction paper and make five boxes. Number the boxes one through five and put a date on the top of the strip. Have Rachel check off a number when she completes a task. Make sure the task is something she can complete to ensure the cueing system works. At first, reward her for completing two out of five tasks. Slowly increase the eligibility for reward to three out of five, until she is able to complete all five tasks. Increase the time increments as the task perseverance increases. Keep the strips in a folder for parent conferences and to show Rachel the progress she is making. If you are ambitious, you can transfer the ratings to an Excel chart.

• Always make certain that there is a beginning, middle, and end to everything Rachel does, even if other classmates do not require that type of instruction. Rachel needs closure every period, every hour, and every day.

• Reduce homework assignments and make clear that she knows when assignments are due in her planner. Due means the day they are due—not *do*! Ensure that the student sitting next to Rachel, in a friendly manner, checks to verify that Rachel knows when assignments are due.

• Always say goodbye to Rachel; if possible, try to make eye contact with her and welcome her back the next day.

• Set up periodic teacher/parent conferences so that the parents clearly understand the importance of the established ground rules and boundaries for Rachel, how you are reinforcing them, and the progress you are making with her.

• Don't give up on Rachel!

Johnny, a third grader, has trouble sitting still in cooperative groups. He becomes the clown and can often be seen jumping up or throwing himself on the ground for attention from his group mates. The teacher reminds Johnny, over and over, what is expected in the group and then uses a warning system with checks for infractions. One check equals a warning, two checks equals no first recess, three checks equals staying in at lunch, and four checks equals a trip to the principal's office. Group work occurs daily in the class and Johnny as a result of this system is either missing a recess or having lunch in the classroom, four out of five days. Rarely does he get four checks. The teacher conferred with other teachers who previously had Johnny in class. Johnny's second-grade teacher did not allow Johnny to participate in groups. She indicated that when other students were in groups, Johnny was given an individual assignment associated with the activity. The teacher then combined Johnny's activity with the associated group. His first-grade teacher allowed Johnny to participate in groups, but let him wander around redirecting him back to the group and monitoring him for task completion. Although this was time consuming, it seemed to work well for Johnny; however, he did not gain task-compliance skills or a sense of perseverance to the task at hand. Both teachers indicated a great deal of frustration with comments such as, "We just learned to put up with him."

Group work for students with ADD presents major challenges for teachers. Since most teachers use some sort of group work or cooperative learning in their classrooms, students must participate to earn a performance letter grade or a grade on a teacher-made rubric. Let's see how we can help Johnny participate in a group so he can derive value out of the experience.

• Assign Johnny to a group with a peer tutor who will keep him on task.

• Have Johnny sit next to the peer tutor.

• Make sure that Johnny has an identified role in the group and an assignment to complete.

• Reduce the activity load for Johnny.

• Allow Johnny to stand up or sit on his legs.

• Reinforce Johnny by name with a very specific comment related to his on-task behavior or his interactions with his group mates. If you must redirect Johnny back on task start with, "Johnny what are you supposed to be doing now? That's right cutting squares and circles. Do you need some help? If not, keep working. Make sure you get one square and one circle done by the time I get back (hand gently on Johnny's arm when you make the final request)." Use a visual cue if needed.

• Make certain that there is a closing activity associated with the group work such as, "What did you accomplish in your groups today?" Have everyone put their heads together and write down one thing the group accomplished on a notepad. Be ready to share.

A student's lack of attention is a bone of contention for most teachers. A student can have attention problems ranging from minor to major. Students with ADD, by the very nature of their disability, have attention problems. However, many students with ADD can selectively attend to things that captivate their attention, such as video games or computer programs. Impulsive behavior such as blurting, interrupting, and over-talking tends to be a pronounced feature of ADD. It is incumbent upon a teacher to discern the difference between a student with a diagnosis of ADD and students who are generally inattentive for one reason or another. The following vignette gives teachers a bird's eye view into the life of Tina and how to best address attention and impulsivity.

Tina, a very active fourth grader has been diagnosed with ADD and takes medicine to counteract some of the effects. The teacher is quite aware of her diagnosis and so that she might be better able to guide and support Tina, she has read her cumulative folder in depth, talked at length with her parents, and talked with other teachers at Willow Elementary School. On a typical day, Tina tends to blurt out answers or requests, gets out of her chair from time to time, and tends to talk over her classmates with a rather loud and imposing voice tone. All of these behaviors, to one degree or another have been identified by her teachers and parents as difficult to handle. Tina's teacher, Ms. Winsome, is a brand new college-minted teacher with some background dealing with ADD students. As a substitute teacher in special education over the last two years, she learned about some positive behavior support approaches that she is employing with Tina. Ms. Winsome is extremely patient and has taken a liking to Tina because, for all of her behavior excesses, Tina has an endearing, humorous, and creative side. Here is what Ms. Winsome has set up for Tina.

- Tina now sits right up front where Ms. Winsome can make eye contact with her and signal her back on task.

- Tina has a behavior chart on her desk marked off by period. She gives herself tally marks when Ms. Winsome tells her to do so. For instance, Ms. Winsome might say, "Good job listening to the directions Tina, give yourself a plus (+) tally mark." At the end of the day Tina's tally marks are counted. At the end of the week, if she has earned enough tally marks she is rewarded with a given set of choices designated by the teacher such as computer time or a homework pass.

- Tina receives a minus (−) tally mark for blurting out an answer or jumping out of her seat. A minus can only be conferred by the teacher and then reviewed with Tina at the end of the day. All tally marks are reviewed by the teacher daily and Tina's (+s) must be 70 percent or better, for example, 3 (−s) to 7 (+s) out of 10 responses in order to receive a reward.

- Ms. Winsome calls on Tina frequently, especially when she is confident Tina knows the answer.

- Ms. Winsome is available to help Tina with a request related to an assignment. Clarifying a direction, cueing Tina back on task, or reteaching all help Tina stay focused on the assignment.

- Ms. Winsome encourages Tina continually, which in turn has led Tina to be more confident and successful in class.

Dealing with students who are overactive and have attention difficulties requires tremendous patience. The strategies and ideas presented in the vignettes can be applied across the board for students exhibiting these behaviors. Once again, structure and routine continue to be the best classroom organizational strategy to offset overactive behaviors.

3

Teacher Self-Esteem

Humane, caring, dedicated, honest, and loving are words that describe most teachers. The work that they do on a daily basis to help children learn borders on saintly. Now, are there some teachers who should have chosen another occupation yet continue to teach? Of course! However, the vast majority of teachers choose teaching because they are drawn to service. Nonetheless, the demands of teaching have placed inordinate stress on even the saintliest among the teaching profession. As a result, teachers' feelings of importance and self-worth can be severely compromised, leading to despair and burnout. Nathaniel Branden's definition of self-esteem from his book *The Art of Living Consciously* captures the essence and importance of self-esteem and what it portends for teachers today. Dr. Branden says "Self-esteem is the disposition to experience oneself as being competent to cope with the basic challenges of life and of being worthy of happiness. It is confidence in the efficacy of our mind, in our ability to think. By extension, it is confidence in our ability to learn, make appropriate choices and decisions, and respond effectively to change. It is also the experience that success, achievement, fulfillment— happiness—are right and natural for us. The survival-value of such confidence is obvious; so is the danger when it is missing" (p. 167).

One can readily see how fulfilling teaching can be and how one's self-esteem, according to Dr. Branden, can be enhanced on a daily basis when children and adolescents are eager to learn. When students make positive comments, it boosts a teacher's feeling of self-efficacy and self-worth, thus creating a sense of achievement and fulfillment that money certainly can't buy. Conversely, when students respond passively or act out, a teacher's sense of self-worth and importance tends to be diminished. Couple that feeling with the pressure for students to meet standards on high-stakes tests, and feelings of inadequacy and loss of control are heightened for teachers. So how do teachers maintain a sense of purpose, esteem, and value for their chosen profession? The question continues to be as perplexing today as it was fifty years ago; however, a few simple tips might aid teachers in maintaining and increasing their self-esteem and their ability to be proactive.

- Set daily goals for yourself. For example, I plan to make an effort to acknowledge student X.

- Establish short-term (weekly) goals such as reviewing your ground rules at least twice in one week, moving around the room more often in order to recognize students for the effort they are putting forth, and greeting students at the door to make them feel welcome.

- Celebrate short-term goals! Bake yourself a cake at the end of the week. Look at yourself in the bathroom mirror, grab your cheeks, and in a loud firm voice say, "Hello Precious, you did a great job this week!"

- Work to make your changes permanent. Ask yourself at the end of each week if you need to keep working on that particular weekly goal. If so, just continue on for another week or two so the changes in your behavior become part of your routine.

- Post this simple reminder somewhere in your room—*Event + Your Response = Consequence*. This notion, articulated by psychologist Virginia Satir, will help you as a teacher realize that whatever event occurs, you can choose how to respond and your choices, positive or negative, will determine the consequences for said choices. For example, a parent makes a seemingly negative comment about one of your teaching strategies—the event. You have a choice to get upset, tell everyone in the teachers' lounge that this parent is on your case (negative response), or call the parent up, discuss the manner in a calm fashion, and review the allegation in order to find a better way to serve her and her child (positive response). Complaining to your colleagues usually results in the consequence of becoming more upset, disappointed, and feeling angry and frustrated. On the other hand, by calling the parent and taking a proactive stance to rectify the issue, you most likely will feel pretty good about yourself. Nine times out of ten, the comment was innocuous and the intent was not meant to demean you or criticize your teaching.

- Teaching can be very isolating and disempowering. Think about it. You have a bad day, which turns into a bad week, which invariably means less sleep and more stress on the weekend. Now you start the week fatigued and the same pattern occurs again. This is how burnout happens—slowly day after day, week after week; burnout does not happen all of a sudden. So to ensure that you continue to enjoy teaching, it is imperative that you connect with your colleagues and share what is happening to you. Commiserate with your colleagues and be open to some of their suggestions in order to make your life as a teacher more pleasant. Be mindful that the *blow-up, give-up* response lurks around every corner (see this chapter). When you feel discouraged or beat down, you are more prone to blame the students, then blame the parents, and then blame the community. Blaming the administration usually is part of a teacher's blaming repertoire. If truth be told, the proverbial finger should be pointed at *you* when the blaming starts. Once again, remember to talk things over with your colleagues. A few words of encouragement from them may be all you need to turn things around.

- Post *Act Positive, Be Positive, Stay Positive* somewhere in your classroom, preferably on your desk. Placing it in an area that you notice each day improves your chances of having a positive, uplifting attitude throughout the day. Remember what goes around comes around—acting positive brings more positive energy your way.

- Find time to relax. Dr. Herbert Benson, in his national bestseller *The Relaxation Response*, clearly articulates the benefits of relaxation. Dr. Benson states that for relaxation to really have an effect on your mind and body, it must be done on a daily basis. There must be some ritual to it. Saying a prayer over and over for 5 to 10 minutes, visualizing yourself in a positive environment, such as the mountains or the beach, or doing some form of stretching (yoga) actually changes your brain chemistry and helps you maintain and improve your health. Teaching can be stressful, so finding time each day to relax undoubtedly benefits you. A calmer, more-centered you equates to more patience and understanding—virtues that certainly resonate with children.

Teachers must be aware of their behavior at all times when interacting with their students. As caretakers and salient role models, what you say and do gets marked down in a student's mental record book. They expect you to act and behave in an emotionally mature manner. Let's take a look at some common behavior traps that teacher's fall into when student behavior presents formidable challenges.

Authoritarian or Passive (Blow-Up or Give-Up) Responses by Teachers

William Glasser, the famous psychiatrist and author of *Choice Theory* said, "If you want to change attitudes start with a change in behavior." That is, if you want students to feel empowered then your behavior as a teacher needs to be positive, respectful, courteous, and genuine. Does that mean every minute of every day? Well just about. Of course, there will be down days where it will take a herculean effort just to show up, hang in there, and make it to the end of the day.

A teacher having a bad day is quite different than the teacher behaviors Lee and Marlene Canter observed when visiting schools. They noticed that many teachers were unable to control undesirable behavior in their classrooms, thus losing control of the classroom and invariably becoming more authoritarian and controlling to quell the disruption. Through the program described in their book, *Assertive Discipline: Positive Behavior Management for Today's Classroom*, they help teachers gain confidence in dealing with student behavior. William Glasser, Lee and Marlene Canter, and numerous other theorists and practitioners offer sage advice and training to help teachers control their emotions in order to deal effectively with student misbehavior. Upon careful reading of these authors, it can be seen that teacher disposition plays a major part in classroom management. As indicated, there will be bad days, but those days will be few and far between when you as a teacher exercise control over your behavior, while at the same time maintaining a healthy respect for your students. So, let's take a look at some examples of how you might respond as a teacher and how that might impact student behavior. In doing so, you can begin to make positive choices for yourself and your students.

To empower students, teachers must first look at their own behavior to ascertain if indeed their actions may be causing the very behavior problems they would like to eliminate. In many classes, there are students who tax teacher patience and frustrate efforts to assist, understand, or tolerate them. The behavior of these students can result in a teacher experiencing feelings of instant frustration, disappointment, worry, helplessness, and inadequacy. Often these feelings turn into reactions of anger, sarcasm, revulsion, or abandonment.

Teachers can improve their own behavior by

(a) anticipating those student behaviors that give rise to undesirable personal responses—be proactive; and

(b) creating and practicing a plan that includes more appropriate and helpful responses in the face of "hot button" student behaviors.

When teachers are faced with challenging student behavior they often respond ineffectively by yelling, ridiculing, making smart comebacks, making embarrassing comments, nagging, ignoring, threatening, arguing, griping, or lecturing students. Teachers tend to *blow-up or give-up*, caught in a cycle of authoritarian (fight or punish) to non-authoritarian (passive or flight) behavior. Aggressive behavior often leads to passive behavior and vice versa. It becomes a perpetual see-saw experience until teachers learn how to manage their behavior in an appropriate and positive manner.

When teachers are authoritarian and use punishment, the following effects can occur:

- Students are not taught what they should do, only what not to do.
- Students and teachers are unable to establish positive, caring relationships due to frequent negative, punitive interactions.
- Students get attention for misbehavior, and over time, students learn to misbehave to get attention.

Typical student results to the *fight or punish* style of teacher interaction are as follows:

- Hostility
- Resistance
- Indifference (low self-esteem or I-don't-care attitude)

When teachers adopt a submissive or passive style of behavior it can interfere with building positive student/teacher relationships; teach students to display inadequacy or an "I-can't-do-it attitude"; and promote immature, verbal responses by both the student and teacher.

Typical student results to the *flight or passive* response style of interaction are as follows:

- Insecurity
- Demand
- Dependency
- Inadequacy (Low self-esteem)

What are some of the annoying behaviors that cause teachers to blow-up or give-up?

- Verbal and physical abuse of another student
- Word and mind games to avoid an issue, for example, "That's not what you said" or "I didn't hear you"
- Intentional disrespect—spitting at or spitting right in front of you, lying, destruction of property
- Excessive use of vulgar or sexually explicit language
- Refusal to do what is asked or challenging you
- Getting in your personal space
- Unmotivated to work
- Inattentive behavior—looks around, talks
- Speaking when the teacher is speaking
- Getting the last word in
- Bad attitude—"whatever" or "so"
- Racial remarks—openly or quietly
- Pouting, whining, tantrums
- Sarcastic remarks or comebacks
- Ridiculing another student

When annoying student behavior occurs, handling oneself in a mature and responsible manner requires a balanced approach to the situation. The annoying behavior can push you into blowing up or just giving up and it is at that very moment you have a choice of how to respond. Instead of fighting or throwing in the towel you can and must act maturely and calmly. Of course, being proactive and having a sense of which students push your buttons and when predictable student misbehavior might occur is your best line of defense against annoying behavior. A few sensible tips will help you stay balanced and in control.

Sensible Tips

Your attitude and perceptions impact your expectations of your students and your reactions toward them. In order for a teacher to create positive rapport with students (knowing well in advance annoying behaviors will occur) you can

- Set the tone—greet students, welcome them, and be available, positive, and proactive. When a student is angry or frustrated over an issue, don't argue or try to convince *him or her* to hear an alternative decision. This tends to create more distress. Just *listen*, restate what you heard, and then schedule a time to discuss the issue later.

- Pause before you pounce—count to ten, walk away, and "get a grip."
- Set personal goals to control your *fight or flight* response to challenging student behaviors.
- *Plan ahead* for behavioral needs of students.
- Request help when needed and seek opinions and ideas from others.
- Generate a number of solutions and implement strategies for improvement.
- Leave your prejudices at home—for example, thoughts such as kids are lazy, unmotivated, stupid, can't do anything right, "kids today."
- Carefully control the structure of your room from the desk placement to the organization of materials.
- Give students an *obnoxious* amount of praise and encouragement.
- Put aphorisms up on the board frequently, for example, "If it's believable—it's achievable," "Every attempt is a victory," and "Everything, and I mean *everything* you do counts."
- Stress cooperation not competition to give students a voice in their education.
- Focus on creating caring, respectful relationships among all students and teachers. For example, with your input have your upper elementary and junior high school students create the rules or classroom expectations.
- Structure instructional activities to ensure a "no fail" situation.
- Determine antecedents or what might precipitate inappropriate behaviors, such as waiting in line, difficulty of a task, too much homework, and then remove them.
- Have a sense of humor and appreciation for the developmental level of your students. This is especially important if you teach junior high school.

Some students may require mental health interventions that address long-range issues involving home life, emotional disturbance, and other life challenges. This is especially true for adolescents. Make sure you contact the school counselor for assistance when student behavior appears to be more of a clinical issue and outside the realm of your professional expertise. These students often require more intensive services from school counselors or special education personnel. These skilled professionals can devise behavioral plans with you as well as provide additional in-class support.

Awareness of the annoying behaviors that particularly upset you is the first step in changing how you respond to students who "get under your skin." By analyzing one's behavior (authoritarian or passive) and reflecting on the consequences of one's actions (blowing up, giving up) teachers can make choices to enhance the emotional health of the students in their class or classes. Too often, there is a tendency to blame the student for behavioral problems when in fact the teacher may have inadvertently triggered the behavior by not creating a classroom structure with clear ground rules and expectations. Interestingly, everything you do in the class matters and students closely monitor your behavior. They notice everything, so it is incumbent upon you to bring your best self to your classroom or educational setting everyday. Remind yourself to think positive thoughts about your students, act positively toward them, and most importantly, take care of yourself so you can continue to be positive.

Part I also includes *Nine Features for Student Empowerment*, elaborating on some of the general ideas and sensible tips included in this chapter. It provides teachers with tools to gain and maintain classroom control, while at the same time supporting the emotional growth and well-being of their students. It also offers students the opportunity to become more responsible for their behavior, in and outside of the classroom.

4

Teaching and Rewarding Responsible Behavior

How often have you heard students say, "He made me do it," "It wasn't my fault," "She was driving and that's why I'm late to school—honest," "My printer was out of ink," "My alarm didn't go off in time," and "My cell phone fell in the toilet and that's why I couldn't call you." All the aforementioned statements are built around excuses and blame, rather than owning up to one's missteps. Taking responsibility for one's actions and feelings can be a daunting task for many students. Pointing the finger at others seems to pay off either by delaying, lessening, or removing the consequence—in the short run. However, in the long run irresponsible behavior (blaming and excuses) finally catches up to a person. And when it does, the direct consequences meted out can be swift and firm. So it is incumbent upon teachers to create a classroom culture that expects students to act responsibly. To do so, teachers must afford students time to practice irresponsible and responsible behavior in a nonthreatening manner. Teachers can provide common examples of a situation and students can role-play responsible and irresponsible actions. For example, in Mrs. Ortiz's fourth-grade class Jennifer and Tomas sometimes push each other in a playful manner. The teacher has chosen to ignore what she perceives to be playful behavior. However, one day Tomas pushes Jennifer harder than usual and she tumbles over a desk and lands in the lap of another student who ends up jamming his pencil into his hand. The injured student (Henry) yells out in pain and then gets up and confronts Tomas, calling him a negative name that the whole class hears and reacts to with a big *ooh*! At that point, the teacher intercedes and implores the students to tell her what's going on. Tomas immediately blames Henry who in turn blames Tomas. Jennifer says nothing until called upon and then blames Tomas. Tomas says that Jennifer pushed him first and if she hadn't then the whole thing would never have happened. As you can readily see from this example, blaming and making excuses rolls off the student's tongues with ease. The teacher can use this situation to role-play how the students should act by asking the following questions: "What happened?" When you answer this question make sure you start with an "I" statement and tell me what happened in just a few words. The teacher asks all three students the same question. Subsequently, she asks the students, one by one, to tell how they could have handled the situation differently. Each student is allowed around 30 seconds—as long as there is no blaming. At that time, she makes the determination if a negative consequence is appropriate or that owning up to the behavior is enough. She also uses the conflict resolution strategies found in this book in Chapter 6, under the heading Conflict Resolution.

Afterward, the teacher debriefs the role play with the class, discussing the effects of the behavior—student injury, the ensuing hurt feelings, and finally the loss of valuable learning time. She indicates that incidents and situations like the one they just role-played will happen in real life and that she doesn't expect the students to act or react to each situation perfectly. However, she does expect them to learn from their behavior and realize that there are consequences for behaving irresponsibly. She also might stress that when you make positive choices, it eliminates the need to defend inappropriate or negative choices. As a result, owning up to one's behavior ("I did it, it was my fault, and I take responsibility") then becomes a common practice in the classroom, whether for minor infractions or major rule-breaking. The following activities teach about responsibility and are aimed at helping students make constructive choices.

- Have one half of the class stand on one side of the room each holding a piece of paper with the word *Response* written on it. Have the other half of the class receive a piece of paper with the word *Ability* on it. Tell the students to find a person with the word *Response* and a person with the word *Ability*. The ground rules for this group activity can include many variables: Commingle the sexes, mix the races, partner with new associates, and other considerations the teacher may want to establish as activity essentials. Following the ground rules of this activity encourages students to take responsibility for their behavior. If the students are unable to comply with the ground rules then have a preselected list of pairs to move the activity along. Once the students are matched up, have them talk with each other about what the two words mean separately and then what it means when they are combined. Ask the students to talk about when and how people use the word responsibility. Also have them discuss how parents and teachers use the word responsibility and what message it usually conveys to them. Then come back together as a group and ask students to share some of their ideas about the word responsibility. Jot their thoughts down on the board. Share your definition and how you would like responsible behavior to be manifested in your room.

- Provide opportunities for students to role-play common situations in order to learn how to take responsibility for their behavior. Make sure to use everyday classroom examples. The students should role-play irresponsible behavior blaming and making excuses and then role-play using responsible statements, which include "I" statements and short explanations of how the situation could have been handled differently. Apply consequences as appropriate, so students understand that there can be minor to major costs associated with acting irresponsibly.

- Play the "It ain't fair game" with your students. The students must blame the teacher using the phrase, "It ain't fair," for everything from grades, to favoritism, to being too strict, to being too lax, to giving way too much homework. Have the students generate an "It ain't fair" list and then see them come to the quick realization that the word *it* is aimed at blaming someone or something other than oneself. Ask the students to figure out a way to turn "It ain't fair" into a more responsible statement. Have them discuss why they feel that things aren't fair and what is a more responsible way to communicate that feeling. This activity is excellent for fourth grade through high school and is especially applicable at the junior high school level.

- Have students pay attention to their behavior for one period and then report what they noticed with another peer or in a small group. Common behaviors might include staying on task, following directions, transitioning from one activity to another, talking with neighbors. The students can then report to the class on the appropriateness or inappropriateness of their behavior.

- Create a *Cop-out Hall of Fame*. Students write down all of their favorite cop-outs on a big piece of butcher paper that the teacher tacks up in a corner of the room. When students make excuses or cop-outs, the teacher can then point to the *Cop-out Hall of Fame* and have the student add it to the list. The teacher can just refer the students to the posted list if they try to use a cop-out that has already been recorded. The teacher can say, "That's a good cop-out, but I think it's already on the list. Why don't you go and check." The teacher can playfully praise students for coming up with a great cop-out. Caution here! Watch out for being too playful, or the zany to the profane cop-outs can spin the class out of control rather quickly.

- Have students fold a piece of paper lengthwise down the middle (like a hot dog), and on one side put the word *responsible* and on the other *irresponsible*. Ask the students to write down as many irresponsible statements they can think of. Give them a few examples, such as "the dog ate my homework" to stimulate their thoughts. After the students have jotted down their irresponsible statements, have them change the statements by putting the pronoun "I" in front of all the statements and then transfer the phrase to the *responsible* side of the paper. Have the students join in small groups with kids they don't ordinarily hang out with, and then have them share their statements with each other. Have each group share their best irresponsible statement and then have them repeat it with "I" in front of it. This is a fun activity reinforcing the notion of taking responsibility for one's actions.

• Stephen Glenn, author of *Raising Self-Reliant Children in a Self-Indulgent World: Seven Building Blocks for Developing Capable Young People,* developed a process of how to share and own up to one's feelings. Instead of hiding or running from your feelings or saying something inappropriate, Dr. Glenn suggested filling in the following sentence starter—*I Feel___About___Because____.* For instance, I feel angry about the comment you just made about my hair because even though you were teasing, my feelings were hurt by what you said. Have students practice using the sentence starter—*I Feel___About___Because___* with a few scenarios that you provide. Make certain that you, as the teacher, share a few of your feelings using the phrase prior to the students completing the activity. Remember feelings, though seemingly innocuous to one student, can trigger strong reactions in other students. Owning up to one's feelings does not come easily for many students, so make certain that you control this activity by giving the students a few simple ideas to fill in the blanks. Make sure to keep this activity light, reinforcing the importance of starting each sentence with "I." It is very easy to blame others for your feelings, so starting with "I" reduces that temptation. This activity must be utilized with a developmentally appropriate group of students. Fourth grade through high school works best.

EVENT + RESPONSE = CONSEQUENCE

Teaching students about responsibility and then rewarding them for taking responsibility for their actions and feelings is the first step in helping students realize that they can make choices about how to behave. Cementing the notion that blaming and making excuses constitutes irresponsible behavior and then practicing responsible behavior can be an eye opener for many students. Once they derive an understanding of the concept of responsibility and it becomes a part of their vernacular and interaction with one another, then the teacher can challenge students to consider an advanced level of *choice-making.* This advanced level of consequential behavior choices encourages and teaches students how to respond appropriately to events that happen in their daily lives. It is also a good lesson for teachers to learn as well. Let's see how it works for both students and teachers.

Family psychotherapist and author Virginia Satir's clever idea (Event + Response = Consequence) speaks to the power that individuals have to make choices that affect their well-being. Dr. Satir acknowledges the fact that there will always be events that stir emotions both positively and negatively. Using Satir's model, students and teachers can begin to *step back* and realize they have the power to choose how to respond to any occurrence or event in their classroom. The way they respond leads to a consequence, which can be either positive or negative for the student and the teacher. For example, Amy passes a note to Leandra accusing Shirley of trying to steal her boyfriend Fernando (*Event*). Leandra confronts Fernando and Shirley in third period and reads both of them the riot act (*Response*). Shirley is caught off guard and responds with a few terse words of her own (*Another Response*). Fernando tries to calm the disagreement by explaining to Leandra that he and Shirley were talking about trying to put a study group together with two other students in the class for an exam they both have to take. He tells Leandra to cool off and walks back to his seat (*Another Response*). Leandra is still fuming and doesn't know whom to believe, Amy or Fernando (*Consequence*). As you can see, the *event* (Amy indicting Shirley) gave way to a *response*, *another response*, and then frustration and anger on the part of all parties involved. This, in turn, led to a *consequence* (Leandra's mistrust of Amy and Fernando), and finally on the part of all involved, led to hurt feelings and the inability to concentrate for the rest of the day. This scenario clearly demonstrates that the way Leandra chose to react to this event led to an inappropriate response and a most upsetting consequence. Leandra could have handled this situation differently by talking it over with Amy after class and finding out the particulars. Leandra probably already has an inkling that Amy has eyes for Fernando and she could then decide if what Amy is saying has any merit or is meant to drive a wedge between her and Fernando. This sign of maturity on Leandra's part comes from understanding how events can lead to misinterpretation and unfavorable responses. Students always have a choice of how to respond to the countless number of events that happen throughout the day. Sometimes students crave the drama and are sparked by the attention. However, most students would prefer a more balanced approach to situations. Teaching students how to react responsibly to events can be affirming and empowering.

The following example shows how a teacher responds inappropriately to an event. A student pushes another student in line (*Event*). The teacher responds by getting upset and pulling the child to the back of the line (*Response*). The student quietly curses and then bumps a student on purpose in the back of line (*Consequence*—anger on the part of the perpetrator and anger from the bumped student toward the perpetrator). The teacher bristles and in an angry tone the child gets both a double check on the board (*Response*) and is required to eat lunch in the classroom with the teacher (*Consequence*). The error and unfortunate consequence in this instance is that the teacher is also punished by staying in class for lunch. This situation could have been handled very differently by clarifying the ground rules for lining up and reinforcing boundaries for personal space. Teachers must anticipate problems. This child most likely has a bit of a history of challenging behaviors; therefore, responding in a more appropriate calm and collected manner increases the likelihood that a consequence will be appropriately meted out.

By employing the simple $E + R = C$ equation, teachers can be proactive rather than reactive (*blowing-up, giving-up*) leading to a healthier and more empowering environment for students. The simple realization that a person is no longer controlled by events that happen but can choose how to respond to those events is a powerful insight.

E + R = C ACTIVITIES

Teacher tacks up a poster with E + R = C in the room as a reminder that you can always make a choice of how to respond. The teacher clearly, in big bold letters, spells out the equation. On the top of the poster the teacher states the quote by the author: *You Always Have a Choice—Make Good Ones for You and Others* (see Appendix 1).

Have students generate a list of common events (developmentally appropriate for the grade level) that cause inappropriate responses, and the resulting consequences. Students can role-play negative responses and the likely consequences. Next, have them role-play how to choose a different, more measured and positive response to the event.

Students can talk about bullying and how E + R = C is a reality at their school. Once again have them look at bullying events, the common responses, and the consequences for that type of behavior. Make certain the students use the equation to take a good, hard look at the most severe consequence of bullying (suicide). This activity is very appropriate for upper elementary through high school.

Students work in pairs to identify occasions where the teacher was reactive to an event and chose a response that was inappropriate. This is a fun non-threatening activity and is an absolute blast for students. The teacher does need to be ready to confront some of his or her own behavior that at times may have been irresponsible.

CHOICE ARCHITECTURE— RIGGING THE EVENT

In the best seller *Nudge*, economists Richard Thaler and Cass Sunstein reinforce Satir's notion of choice, albeit with a slightly different bent. They posit that choice can be architecturally designed to move people in the direction to which they were already headed. They coined the term "choice architecture" which is simply a way of designing the environment so that people make positive choices without realizing they are doing so. Choice architecture is a way of rigging the event so that a predictable response occurs with positive consequences. According to Thaler and Sunstein, you nudge people to make the correct response. A good example of choice architecture centers on a fairly common activity, ATM transactions. You may not realize that before the ATM spits out your money, the machine forces you to take out your card. Prior to this choice architecture, people were constantly leaving their cards in the ATM because the money was offered first. You may have been one of those unlucky people who realized (usually after driving away) that you left your ATM card behind, drove back to retrieve it, only to find that the machine had gobbled it up. Well that no longer happens because of choice architecture—you have to remove your card before you get the prize—your money; hence a positive outcome or response and a nudge to make the right choice.

Now how can choice architecture help teachers better manage their classrooms? Let's take a look at ways teachers can design some choices to move students in the direction that is not only good for them, but helps make the class run more efficiently and effectively. Let's imagine a teacher meets and greets his students at the door prior to the start of class for the day, shakes their hands, and then says in an upbeat tone, "Have a great day, great to have you in class!" Variations on the salutation might include, "You've got what it takes. Have a wonderful day." "I love that smile, looks like it's going to be a fabulous day for learning." By doing this, the teacher not only sends a positive, empowering message to the students but designs a choice in the greeting response about the tenor of the day. Of course, the student can disregard the salutation and act out; however, by rigging this event the likelihood is that students will enjoy the class session and their chances for having a "wonderful day" increase. A nudge.

Another way a teacher can employ choice architecture is by placing two bins on the top of his or her table with signs prominently displayed, reading *homework* and *no homework*. The student now has a choice: should I drop a piece of paper in the *no homework* bin and have to explain why I have no homework or not put anything in that bin. By architecturally designing the choice, at the very least the teacher moves the student to consider the consequences of turning or not turning in his or her homework. In this example, the teacher is nudging the students in the direction of completing their homework without suffering the consequences of a poor grade resulting from not complying with the homework policy. It also relieves the teacher from constantly reminding students to turn in their homework.

Fred Jones in his excellent resource entitled *Tools for Teaching* turns the tables on the "grandma's rule" with a group management system he titles Preferred Activity Time or PAT. With *grandma's rule* you first do something and then you receive something in return. For instance, if you clean your room, you can go out to play. In behavioral terms this is known as contingency management; the reward is contingent upon meeting the demands of a stated behavioral request. With PAT the students receive a given number of minutes, say 20 minutes per week, which can be used or saved to apply to fun yet instructional, sanctioned activities. They do not have to earn the minutes. They can save up their minutes for a couple of weeks to participate in a longer activity, for example a video or another fun, agreed-upon activity. Now here is the catch. If you are off task, or bend, or abuse the classroom rules, the teacher subtracts seconds or sometimes up to a minute or so off your PAT. The teacher stands motionless in front of the class with a stopwatch or some timepiece and clicks it while waiting for the students to either get back on task or stop the undesirable behavior. Once students are back on task or the behavior has stopped, the teacher subtracts seconds or minutes from the PAT and then continues with the lesson. The teacher rigs the event. Instead of the proverbial "you do this and you get that," or traditional behavior management plans built on rewards and punishments, the teacher turns it over to the students to manage their own behavior. They clearly exercise a choice. PAT is designed to nudge them to act and respond in a positive manner without them really being aware that their behavior is being directed.

To nudge students to respect others, reduce put-downs, and to develop virtuous behavior, teachers might want to consider putting a big sign up in the front of the class titled *Random Acts of Kindness*. The teacher establishes a *Random Acts of Kindness Box* stationed somewhere obvious in the room where students can put a slip of paper with their name on it to indicate what act of kindness they performed. They can also just put their name on the slip without discussing what they actually did. The teacher, at a designated time during the week, pulls a slip from the box and calls on the student to discuss what she or he did to help others. The teacher then guides a class discussion related to that particular student's act of kindness. The teacher can elect to open up the discussion for the whole group or in small groups with some discussion prompts. If students get really involved, they can establish a *Random Act of Kindness* blog.

The teacher needs to jot down a few ground rules for the *Random Acts of Kindness* nudge, such as be mindful that helping others truly helps you become a better person. Remind the students that if they just stick their name in the box to be funny or to draw rude pictures they defeat the purpose of what acting kindly toward others really means. Ground rules can also be developed for the corresponding class discussion.

Nudging students to make choices they would have made anyway requires a bit of creativity on the part of the teacher. These examples provide fodder for thought. When teachers chat with each other, amazing creative ideas spring forth. Though this is a new concept and may be unfamiliar territory for teachers, as soon as they start rigging an event through choice architecture, students unwittingly behave in more positive and endearing ways.

5

Responsible Instruction

I was in a small rural school recently that had two classrooms divided by bookcases and a makeshift screen. Although the teacher I was visiting was exemplary, the teacher next to her was berating a few of her students working in a small group. Although it did not seem to disturb the teacher or the students in the classroom I was visiting, it was loud enough for me to hear. I jotted down a few statements made by Ms. Frustrated.

That's wrong!

No, no it's not that!

You haven't done anything.

You don't do it that way.

What are you doing?

I didn't say it was right, *did I?*

You multiplied wrong, what's wrong with you?

I'm not going to ask again.

We're waiting for you, put that down.

I'm not telling you again, there should be no talking.

Stop, you're not done yet.

For students to learn responsible behavior, teachers must be positive role models. The aforementioned statements clearly show a teacher frustrated with her students. These messages undermine elements so essential to learning such as student interest and risk-taking. Over the last few years, researchers such as Robert Marzano, Grant Wiggins, and Anita Archer have written books and provided professional development seminars to help teachers improve their instruction (see annotated Bibliography). With improved and targeted instruction, classroom management becomes less of an issue because students are actively engaged. Teachers who become frustrated, such as the teacher using the disempowering demands and comments above, have either not prepared the lesson well, don't know how to deliver powerful and engaging instruction, or have just plain given up. Teachers who truly want to magnify responsible instruction in their classroom use student-centered techniques to encourage inquisitiveness and critical thinking. They also provide direct and explicit instruction so that students know what is expected and how to do the task at hand. Teachers guide instruction, drive for mastery, and provide corrective feedback in a meaningful way, so students feel empowered, capable, and competent.

Responsible instruction means that the teacher makes adjustments in delivery to meet the needs of students in order to ensure that learning takes place and student effort is rewarded and honored. In this type of classroom, one can expect numerous opportunities for peer interaction, cooperative groups, station teaching (where students move from one instructional opportunity to another on a scheduled basis), positive student conversations, and loads of encouragement from the teacher. Responsible instruction means that teachers check for understanding on a continual basis, using formative assessment techniques such as Exit Slips, where students let the teacher know what they learned and what they still don't understand or are confused about. The teacher then can use the information to reteach the concept the next day or provide additional instruction if needed. In responsible teaching, every minute of the day one can find students actively engaged—their minds turned on by responding to loads of hands-on activities.

When teachers make instruction a priority and create an environment where learners become the focal point, learners can take full advantage of the afforded opportunity; most notably, the results are that behavior problems are reduced, learning and attention increases, and both teachers and students feel empowered. I call this type of teacher a *WAHOO* teacher—a teacher who is flexible, creative, patient, has a good sense of humor, relates what is being taught to student experiences, and most importantly, has an enduring love for the students. You can find more *WAHOO* teachers in our schools than the teachers exemplified by the irresponsible behavior of Ms. Frustrated.

RESPONSIBLE INSTRUCTION

In the same illustrative pattern, the following two vignettes show and contrast differences in instructional style and intention. Mrs. Darling always encourages her students to do their best. Her lessons are well-planned with numerous opportunities for student interaction. She frequently uses the technique of talking through a problem so the students can see how she might figure things out;

this is called a *think-aloud*. She uses peer-response partners to ensure that the students elicit responses rather than simply guess at the correct response or try to read her mind in hopes of getting the right answer. After she covers the content of a lesson, Mrs. Darling's students respond chorally to questions. For choral responding she says, "One and all," and then puts one finger above her head signaling students to *wait* then blinks ten fingers to signal that *all* should respond together. Students work cooperatively in groups for basic classroom assignments and for large projects. She continually assesses the groups using quick writes, quizzes, and a fun game she calls, *Content-u-Love-a-Lot*—a game where students work in triads to figure out questions related to the content she just covered in class. The games come in all forms: from jeopardy, to crosswords, to physical responses like jumping up and down with the answer. It is not unusual to find students in her class hopping around while playing Content-u-Love-a-Lot. Students always fill out an Exit Slip prior to leaving class with a couple of questions she has printed on the slip—What did you learn? What was confusing? What can I improve upon? She collects all Exit Slips and then collates the responses in an Excel chart (takes less than 5 minutes). When she doesn't have time to enter them into her Excel chart, she reviews them to gauge student understanding to decide whether to reteach or to move onto the next lesson. Mrs. Darling strongly believes in student voice and holds classroom meetings (see Chapter 6) to handle disputes. She has classroom managers (see Chapter 6) for most tasks in the classroom in order to give students a sense of leadership and ownership in the class. She is proactive, has high yet realistic expectations, and is an excellent role model; most of all, Mrs. Darling cares deeply for her students and, as a result, her students care deeply for her. Her quality instruction reduces behavior problems because students are so engaged, enthralled, and empowered.

IRRESPONSIBLE INSTRUCTION

Mr. Category has taught eighth-grade math at the same school for 23 years. He prides himself on being a no-nonsense kind of teacher. "Either the kids like me or they don't," he will often say in a booming bravado voice. He developed his syllabus years ago and only changes the dates each year. It is as if students are freeze-dried in a frame he created two decades ago. Students put up with Mr. Category and the school administration and others in his department have learned to live with his taciturn manner. His instruction consists of showing the students a few formulas on the board and then handing out worksheets. When the students complete their worksheets they place them in a wire basket on a table labeled "Here Dummies" with a dummy he props up next to the sign. The administration loathes the sign; however, Mr. Category continues to use it year after year. He laughs it away at parent conferences and open houses telling parents that the sign doesn't bother his students and, matter of fact, the sign works—there are only a small number of students who fail to put their worksheets in the wire basket. When students complete their worksheets they can work at their desks quietly. Most students, out of sheer boredom, while away the time doodling, daydreaming, or sleeping. It is probably safe to say that fewer students cause problems in Mr. Category's class because he can be downright mean.

KEYS POINTS FOR RESPONSIBLE INSTRUCTION

A proactive teacher thinks about how to make instruction fun and meaningful. Differentiating instruction to meet the needs of all diverse learners in a classroom empowers the students. Actively engaged students require less classroom management strategies and behavior control methods and reflect the time dedicated teachers put into lesson and unit design (which invariably means working overtime). Let's look at the key components of responsible instruction.

- Plan lessons/units well in advance.
- Work with grade-level teams to ensure similar content is being covered.
- Work across grade-level teams to integrate curriculum.
- Start each lesson on time (no excuses).
- Associate a warm-up activity with the lesson or as a review.
- Activate prior knowledge or preassess what the students already know about the content.
- Instruct using visuals such as document cameras, SMART Boards, overheads, and white board.
- Ensure students understand the big ideas, vocabulary, and important concepts, dates, formulas, and strategies using think-alouds and choral response. Use the *5 and 1* strategy—5 minutes of instruction to 1 minute of students processing the information in pairs or triads.
- Plan to use examples and nonexamples to teach a concept to students. A nonexample has a few elements missing from the correct example. A nonexample (where a few critical attributes of a sentence are missing) looks something like this:

the animal rescue agency ran an advertizement in the local newspaper for three voluteers to help clean cages and feed sick animal's

You write this sentence on the white board and invite a student or students to make the necessary changes to correct the sentence. You then check with the class and they can give the students a thumbs-up, or thumbs to the side (they missed one), or thumbs down. The correct sentence is as follows:

The animal rescue agency ran an advertisement in the local newspaper for three volunteers to help clean cages and feed sick animals.

- Use peer-response partners frequently during the lesson to ensure students understand concepts. For example, if partner A turns to partner B and explains the definition of *photosynthesis* then both are vested in learning the concept.

- Create cooperative learning groups for students to work interdependently on an assignment associated with the content. Assign roles and make sure students are accountable.
- Check for understanding—move around the room reteaching or giving prompts to help students understand the lesson, use white boards for students to jot down answers or work out problems. Have quick writes, short daily quizzes, games, and anything you can think of to make sure students get the gristle, fat, and the meat of instruction, for example, games such as *Ticket Out* (give them a problem that you just covered as their ticket out of the class that day) and *Exit Slips*.
- Close the lesson in a timely fashion. Leave 5 minutes for review at the end of the lesson. Here is where you can use your Ticket Out or Exit Slip.
- Gather materials and have students write needed information in their daily planners.
- Give students a warm and sincere good-bye.

6

Nine Features for Effective Classroom Management and Student Empowerment

This chapter features strategies and ideas for student empowerment and includes nine features which teachers can use to analyze and evaluate their effectiveness as classroom managers. This information is designed to help children become more self-reliant and at the same time make classroom management less burdensome for the teacher.

THE IeAM SYSTEM

I have been in education for over 30 years and I have noticed that successful classroom managers subscribe to a couple of basic principles. They invariably do the following:

1. **Identify** and <u>use</u> a classroom management method that is easy to implement and that fits their individual teaching style;

2. **Establish** clear limits with ground rules for behavior and then follow through consistently throughout the day, week, month, semester, and school year;

3. **Apply** appropriate positive or negative consequences *immediately;* and

4. **Maintain** a consistent, clearly understood approach to classroom management to foster student trust and respect.

These four simple principles (dubbed I*e*AM) guide the best classroom managers. Why? Because for busy teachers, too often sophisticated behavior methods fall by the wayside. Ease of implementation is critical for a classroom teacher. And of course, the behavior method must fit with the teacher's style of teaching. The I*e*AM acronym acts as a handy reminder of what a teacher can do when student and classroom behaviors pose challenges.

Quality instruction hinges on how well you handle yourself and your classroom. By using the I*e*AM system you will have more control and confidence in managing your classroom. A classroom where students know the limits, respond to your requests in a respectful manner, and conduct themselves responsibly is a classroom where learning flourishes. Though challenging at first, identifying the approach that best works for you reaps the most benefits during a lengthy school year. Spending some time musing about what classroom management you want to employ for the group of students you have in that given year gives you a chance to modify approaches that you have used in the past or to change your approach altogether. Once again, the key is to identify a classroom management method or system that resonates with you and that you can consistently implement. Oftentimes, behavior problems occur because of inconsistencies on the teachers' part, not on the students' part.

It must be noted that teachers exemplify different styles of interaction with students. Some teachers feed off of student energy and seem to have boundless energy as well. Others move through the day in a predictable, measured manner while others need a strict adherance to time and schedules. For example, a teacher with a laid-back style may use a classroom management system based on building relationships with students. Talking with students frequently, greeting them at the door, sharing positive comments, and allowing for numerous opportunities for student interaction work well for this type of teacher. This teacher is also comfortable with noise, movement about the classroom, student discussion, and problem solving. Although this style seems *loose*, it might be a good personality fit for this particular teacher. Constant and sustained positive teacher/student interaction marks this teacher's approach to classroom management. Positive reinforcement mitigates the need for negative reinforcement. Students expect the teacher to behave in this manner from day to day and the classroom culture takes on that relaxed character. A teacher with an easygoing nature often opts for building an overall classroom atmosphere that values interpersonal relationships, rather than managing reward systems that require record keeping. Although the I*e*AM system is not as obvious in this example (as it is in the case of clearly designed external reward methods), all of the I*e*AM features are in place and addressed.

Another teacher might use an external reinforcement system such as a checklist for appropriate classroom behavior, for example, supporting behaviors like staying in your seat, bringing materials to class, and waiting your turn in line. Students may then receive a daily or weekly reward contingent upon their individual behavior. For a teacher using a contingency-management system, the features outlined in the I*e*AM system correlate nicely.

For teachers who are comfortable with more intensive monitoring and data recording, a highly structured management system with external reinforcements may be a perfect fit. This teacher might identify a classroom management approach that is highly visible to the students so that they can see their progress and make adjustments to their behavior. Once students become comfortable with the system and recognize that the teacher's approach is consistent and fair then their behavior tends to comply with the established classroom management approach.

Students, for the most part, rely on clear, identified classroom structure with rules and guidelines for behavior. Without structure and classroom behavoiral norms, learning is compromised. Once the teacher recognizes his or her style and then identifies a classroom management approach that complements that particular style, learning flourishes.

The following is an example of a teacher using the I*e*AM system. It should take less than ten minutes to jot the information down using the I*e*AM template found in the Appendix.

Sample I*e*AM System—Mrs. Perez

(I) IDENTIFY: (Mrs. Perez, sixth-grade teacher) The classroom management system I selected was developed by Fred Jones and is titled Preferred Activity Time (PAT). It is easy to implement, fits my style, and will benefit the students I have this year.

(*e*) ESTABLISH GROUND RULES: I give my students 30 minutes of time per week that they control or basically own. I write down 30 minutes on the corner of my white board and then place a border around it. I tell my students that these minutes are theirs to keep; that is, if they behave apppropriately, they can then use whatever time is left at the end of the week for an academically related *free time* activity or they can save the minutes to use for a longer activity, such as a video. But I tell them, there's a catch.

(A) APPLY APPROPRIATE CONSEQUENCES: I then tell them the catch— if they are off task, talking out of turn, fooling around, or out of their seat, I turn on the stopwatch function on my wristwatch and let it run until they are behaving appropriately. As soon as they are behaving in an appropriate manner, I click *stop* on my watch, go over to the board, subtract that time (usually less than a minute) from their free time, and then proceed with my lesson. My students get a clear picture of how much time they have left when I subtract the time. This usually "bums" them out and as a group they tend to start monitoring each other in order to save their PAT.

(M) MAINTAIN: I stay calm and cool and do not negotiate with the students when subtracting time from their PAT. I am super consistent, unmovable, and unshakable. I know they want to keep their PAT and it is up to me to follow through and be consistent.

Sample IeAM System—Mr. Olsen

(I) IDENTIFY: (Mr. Olsen, third-grade teacher) I plan to change my classroom management system over winter break. I visited a class where each student had displayed on the corner of their desktops a period-by-period, weekly check-sheet. My students are pretty diverse this year and I need to introduce a different management system. I think this will work perfectly.

(e) ESTABLISH GROUND RULES: I will make copies of the checksheet for the week and explain and model how to use it. Students on task during a period receive a check. Students can accumulate six checks per day. They can also earn an Olsen "WOW" or a *W*. If they do something extraordinary, like help a classmate struggling with academics, hold the door for a student with disabilities, or share their lunch with a classmate they can mark a *W* next to the period in which they earned it.

(A) APPLY APPROPRIATE CONSEQUENCES: At the end of the day the students add up their checks. I have a notebook and will write down each student's daily score. To receive a *W*, however, is something special and three *W*s gives the student a free homework pass. I then write down a *W* next to their name for that day. Twenty to 30 checks gets you a small bag of popcorn to take home with you on Friday. Below 20 gives you a chance to improve next week.

(M) MAINTAIN: I need to move about the room to get a clear indication of who is, or who is not, on task. I will give out the checks myself or tell the student to give himself or herself a check. I am vigilant about recording scores down daily so students know that I am serious. I will counsel with students who find it difficult to reach between 20 and 30 points to ascertain if I am favoring certain students, or not providing enough opportunities for success. This is a big undertaking, but I need to follow this program to bring my class in line. I think there can be variations down the line, for example, peer-to-peer recording of checks.

As you can see, using the IeAM Template to jot down a management approach provides the teacher with a clear and useful action plan. Writing the plan down on paper shows commitment, a sense of purpose, and good intentions on the teacher's part and thus increases the likelihood of a successful outcome. Teachers might consider placing a copy of their IeAM Template on their desks as a reminder.

Teachers may want to post IeAM CAPABLE, or IeAM WITH IT, or any other saying that instantly connects them to the IeAM acronym in a location that they pass by frequently throughout the day. By using the IeAM system, teachers reduce the likelihood that problem behavior escalates or continues.

The next major section, Part II, *Activities to Promote Positive Classroom and Student Behavior,* underscores the importance of teachers using concrete management techniques to develop a supportive and nurturing classroom atmosphere. Part II provides teachers with numerous activities to employ the IeAM system.

DATA COLLECTION

Although the IeAM system works for most students, some students' modus operandi (MO) is to *act out* (defiant, oppositional, aggressive behavior toward the teacher) while other students elect to *act in* (display inadequacy, withdrawal, and defensive behavior). Some students, if things are not going their way, will destroy the game any chance they can. Others become the judge of the game and act above it all. It seems as if these students think that everyone, including the teacher, is less competent and less intelligent than they are. I had a friend who, when he started to lose at Monopoly, would pound the board so hard that money, houses, and cards went flying through the air—his way of destroying the game. For this type of student, teachers can employ some very simple data collection methods to establish when and where the behavior is taking place and who and what might be the cause. Sometimes a simple solution of moving a student to another seat location or moving that student to another teacher for a period or two cures the problem. When the problem belies a simple solution, then finding out what triggers the behavior, when it seems to occur most often, by collecting data and then analyzing the data, helps teachers make an informed choice of how to handle the behavior. Given the busy schedules of teachers usually means that any system that requires keeping notes or data on a particular child can feel like an imposition on their time. Finding and then using a recording form allows the teacher to track and record behavioral occurrences to better address a student's behavioral needs.

According to Ellerd, Harrower, and Powell (2011), a scatterplot (see example) is a method a teacher can use to track occurrences and nonoccurrences of behavior across *routines*, *activities*, and *time periods* while providing a visual display of behavioral patterns. By tracking and recording behavioral occurrences over a few weeks, teachers can ascertain what might be the best solution for a child's behavior pattern. It also reduces the likelihood that a teacher makes inaccurate assumptions about a child and then institutes a behavioral approach that could potentially escalate any behavior issues. A teacher must not underestimate difficult and challenging behavior problems, especially if the behavior problems disrupt the entire class. By taking data and then employing a behavioral approach to deal with the behavior, the teacher effectively sends a clear message to a student—I am in control! Also, data pertaining to difficult students provide valuable information to other teachers and related professionals. By sharing this information at team meetings (grade-level, student-study, or (IEP) individual educational program) a consistent approach can be implemented throughout the school.

Note: It is important to remember that student safety comes first and foremost. If behavior escalates to a point where the teacher does not feel that he or she is in control or feels that the welfare of other students in the class is jeopardized, then the use of the discipline procedures developed for the school (see disciplinary referral in the Appendix) is mandated. A discipline report triggers an automatic contact with the parent.

SCATTERPLOT

Student:	James Joy	**Target Behavior:** *Talking out of turn while poking student next to him*	
Observer:	Mrs. Brightness		
Start Date:	October 1, 2011		
End Date:	October 15, 2011	**Task avoidance, oppositional Behavior:** *Sometimes slams head down on desk and refuses to work*	

Using a scatter plot involves recording the times of the day (and/or activities) in which the behavior does and does not occur to identify patterns that take place over days or weeks.

Time	Activity	Dates											
		10/1	2	3	4	5	8	9	10	11	12	15	16
8:00	Student Arrival												
8:10	Writing												
9:10	P.E./Music												
10:00-11:30	Language Arts	XXX XXXX XXXX	XXX XX	XX X	XX	X	XXX XXX	XXX	XX X	XX	XXX	XX	XX
11:30	Recess												
12:00	Lunch												
12:30	Math												
1:30	Vocab./SSR												
2:00	Sci./Social Studies	O	O	XX	O	O	O	O	XXX	O	O	O	O
2:30	Computer Lab												
3:00	Home												

O = Behavior did not occur, X = Behavior occurred, Blank = Not observed

Source: Bureau of Instructional Support and Community Service, Florida Department of Education. Developed by the staff Positive Behavioral Support (PBS) Project, Department of Child and Family Studies of the Louis de la Parte Institute at the University of South Florida, and funded by the State of Florida.

The teacher observed James in two class sessions over a two-week period. The teacher knew that he was disruptive (talking out of turn and poking the student next to him) in language arts and had a few problems in science, but couldn't quite put his or her finger on why he was misbehaving during those classroom times. What was even more perplexing was the oppositional behavior of slamming his head down on the desk to avoid an activity.

The data kept on James helped the teacher analyze the teaching and make some decisions that would not only help James but the rest of the class. To see if the changes instituted had an effect on James, the teacher continued to use the scatterplot for two more weeks. Most notably, the task-avoidance behavior of slamming his head down on the desk was virtually eliminated.

Using a tally mark for each behavioral occurrence works best; however, some teachers when collecting data on challenging behavior use a system where they wear an apron and transfer paperclips or poker chips from one pocket to another to record the behavior. Do not over analyze! If you notice the behavior occurring just put a tally mark in the appropriate space. After a couple of days you will begin to notice a pattern. At that time, check to see if there are antecedents, for example, if your directions were unclear, the activity started late, there was a change in peer seating, or class intrusions. Continue to take data for at least two weeks to ensure that you have enough information to make competent decisions. Use the information to change your teaching, change your response toward the student, or employ a behavioral activity or approach that speaks to your newfound awareness (see blank scatterplot, Appendix 7).

CLASSROOM PROCEDURES AND ROUTINES CHECKLIST

Several years back, the U.S. Department of Education published a document entitled *5 Ways to Manage a Classroom*. The list of ideas, based on information from research done through the NIE, National Institute of Education (now known as OERI, the Office of Educational Research and Improvement), is as vital today as when it was first written. Clearly defining and teaching classroom procedures and routines cannot be overemphasized. The following two concepts were specifically chosen to introduce this section and to ask teachers to reflect on their classroom management procedures and routines, to fill out a checklist, and to make changes as deemed appropriate.

- **Clearly define classroom procedures and routines**. Students need to know how a teacher expects them to behave and to handle daily routines. It is important that a teacher develop specific rules and procedures before the school year begins. Besides helping a teacher manage a class, well-established procedures help eliminate wasted time. For instance, if a teacher does not have a routine for handling daily, necessary chores such as reporting attendance, checking work, or collecting lunch money then large amounts of time are spent on these tasks rather than on learning.

Teachers need to let students know how they should behave while the teacher is taking care of administrative chores; how they should begin and end classwork; how they should participate during class; or the rules for talking during seatwork. One elementary school teacher, Ms. May, told me that her instructional routines were pretty good in the morning but not so great in the afternoon. I asked her if she experiences more behavior problems in the afternoon. Her immediate answer was *Yes!* At that moment the proverbial light bulb went off in her head, and without hesitation, she said she was going to institute the same instructional routines in the afternoon that she uses in the morning to reduce the afternoon behavioral problems. This "aha" moment is not uncustomary for elementary school teachers. Afternoons often include other academic subjects, such as science and computer lab, which are more interactive. After a long morning of systematic, instructional routines in math and reading even the best teachers tend to relax and stray from classroom procedures and routines. Unfortunately, this tends to work against them as evidenced by this teacher's admission. Managing behavioral problems at the end of the day drains energy from the teacher and creates more work and stress. Better to be unrelenting with instructional routines for the entire day, week, month, and year.

- **Teach students classroom procedures and routines**. Researchers have discovered that, in the early weeks of the school year, effective classroom managers spend a good deal of class time introducing students to rules and procedures. It is important that teachers review daily schedules, lunch and recess breaks, when to sharpen pencils, and when to raise hands. Students should not be expected to learn all of the rules and procedures in one class, especially elementary school students. Expected behaviors and consequences need to be clearly explained, taught, reinforced, and then retaught, just like reading, math, science, and social studies. Here is an example shared by an elementary school teacher. In this example there is a daily schedule and a reward associated with each activity. Each student has a checkbook where they earn individual points that can be accumulated and then cashed in at the classroom store on Fridays. Stickers are used to acknowledge students and stamps are used for completed work and to signal appreciation for a job well done.

Daily Class Procedures	Rewards
Enter classroom by walking and sitting quietly at assigned seat or work station.	Group game during recess.
Have school supplies out and be ready to work.	Group oral appreciation.
Copy notes from the white board when directed.	Oral appreciation, stamps for completed assigned work.
Raise hand from your seat to get help on an assignment or to ask a question related to classwork.	Oral appreciation. Assigned class monitor for a period.
Put your hand on your shoulder if you need to use the bathroom, sharpen pencils, or get classroom resources.	Oral appreciation.
Carry the hall/bathroom pass and sign out and in when hall/bathroom pass granted.	Oral appreciation.
Use school planner to record words of the week every Monday.	Stickers and points in checkbooks for use at Friday store.
Write sentences using new words daily.	Stickers and great work posted on *Student Chart Wall*.

Daily Class Procedures	Rewards
Transition by looking and listening to adults after oral countdown of three, two, one or with three, two, one hand gestures.	On-time release for recess and lunch.
Use computers as directed for research or keyboarding. No food, liquids, or touching of computer screens allowed.	Additional time on computers added during free time.
Walk in a straight line as directed by teachers or other adults when going out for recess or lunch.	Adult encouragement and points in check book.
Stand quietly behind chairs when dismissed from class with desk organized, and area clean.	Line up first based upon compliance and oral appreciation.
Settle disputes by apologizing quickly and sincerely.	Minimum loss of free time and recess time.
Complete and turn in homework.	High fives and points in check book.

Adapted with permission from my friend and colleague, Ricky Thompson, an elementary special education teacher, Gilroy Unified School District, Gilroy, California.

Incorporating Procedures in Your Classroom

Defining and teaching classroom procedures and routines offsets the vast majority of student behavior problems. The *Classroom Procedures and Routines Checklist* offers teachers an opportunity to reflect on their practice which in turn helps to create a positive learning and social environment. It also helps teachers develop and maintain positive relationships with their students. Use the checklist below as a simple reminder to incorporate these ideas in your classroom. Put a check by *YES*, *NO*, or *SORT OF*. If you check *NO* or *SORT OF* for some of the items, then you can start working on improving one or two of those areas. Simply circle the number to the left of the item and then begin to think about or actually change your practice. Once you believe that you have a good handle on the first couple of items that you checked, give yourself a pat on the back. Check the list periodically throughout the semester to see if any other areas pop up and then follow the same steps as indicated above. A quick reminder here—consistency over time equals change in behavior (consistency × time = change). So it is incumbent upon you to check yourself to see if you are following through on areas that you have identified on the checklist. Use some of the strategies in the book to help you improve.

Classroom Procedure and
Routines Checklist for Teachers

1. **Organizational Strategies:** Students are taught organizational strategies including how to use binders or notebooks with calendars to keep track of homework and important dates and are encouraged to have a storage compartment in binders for carrying materials needed including pencils and erasers. These skills are checked and reinforced periodically.

❑ YES ❑ NO ❑ SORT OF

2. **Room Environment:** As the teacher moves throughout the classroom, all of the students can be seen from anywhere in the room. Computers face into the room and are easily monitored. There is an area of the room, "Australia," where a student can choose to go to, if needed, for a cool-off period or just to have some peace and quiet.

❑ YES ❑ NO ❑ SORT OF

3. **Rules/Expectations and Procedures:** Students actively participate in developing the classroom rules and expectations which are then posted and/ or distributed to the students. The rules and expectations are written in a positive tone with no more than five rules or expectations outlined.

❑ YES ❑ NO ❑ SORT OF

4. **Scheduling:** The students have ample time to complete work. Students who finish work early know what task to move onto next and are rewarded for keeping on task.

❑ YES ❑ NO ❑ SORT OF

5. **Transitions:** Transitions are planned and smooth. Students are prepared and know what to expect and how to do their part to help transition smoothly from one task to the next.

❑ YES ❑ NO ❑ SORT OF

6. **Instructional Strategies:** Students are given many strategies to help them solve problems. Strategies are posted, repeated often and printed on their lesson materials to aid in initial learning. Lectures are kept short, practice is monitored, and breaks occur regularly.

❑ YES ❑ NO ❑ SORT OF

7. **Student–Teacher Relationship:** The teacher respects the students and acts accordingly. The teacher shares personal stories, encourages students to share with the class at a suitable time, and models appropriate social interaction behaviors at all times. Students are made to feel a valued part of the class and that what they say and feel matters.

☐ YES   ☐ NO   ☐ SORT OF

8. **Encouraging Independence and Responsibility:** Students are provided with a multitude of choices within lessons and free time. They have jobs or manager roles they can complete with little or no teacher support. There are back-up activities students can choose from, and go on to, when their work is completed.

☐ YES   ☐ NO   ☐ SORT OF

9. **Positive Behavior System:** There is a positive behavior system in place that consistently encourages and rewards positive behavior while discouraging negative behavior. In Part I of the book a number of described activities qualify and reinforce this type of system.

☐ YES   ☐ NO   ☐ SORT OF

The routines and procedures on the classroom checklist function as a general reminder for teachers. Tailoring this checklist by adding more specific procedures to meet the individual student's needs works best. For instance, a routine that seems to work for most teachers is some sort of a signal to gain student attention. Some signals used by effective teachers include using a bell timer, turning on the lights, raising a finger to the lips, and repeating a particular phrase (such as "eyes on me"). It is amazing how a simple signal to gain student attention can be so effective in creating and maintaining a sense of order in the classroom. Having predictable classroom routines and procedures in place, like the signal for attention, means more time for quality instruction.

TEACHER CLASSROOM MANAGEMENT SELF-CHECK

Managing a classroom takes tremendous effort and perserverance on the part of teachers. Ensuring that a classroom has an identified management system (IeAM) in place, some form of data collection process for difficult students, and procedures and routines clearly articluated continues to be of primary importance for well-run classrooms. To be an effective classroom manager requires monitoring student behavior, handling inappropriate behavior promptly and consistently, and planning ahead. These skills are healthy reminders of what good management practice entails. Reviewing a few additional points from the *5 Ways to Manage a Classroom* broadens a teacher's understanding of basic and useful management techniques.

- **Monitor student behavior.** Effective classroom managers are aware of their students' behavior at all times. They know who is working and who is not because they station themselves where they can see all of their students at all times and can scan all parts of the classroom regularly. They let students know they are aware of what is going on. They move around during work and are careful not to become so engrossed with one student that they lose contact with the rest. Research has shown that teachers who successfully manage their classrooms are successful, not because they respond differently to misbehavior than other teachers do, but because they prevent disruptive student behavior from happening by keeping a close eye on their students.

- **Handle inappropriate behavior promptly and consistently.** Careful monitoring allows a teacher to detect inappropriate behavior when it first occurs and, therefore, when it is easiest to correct. If a teacher continually ignores misbehavior, it is likely to increase. An effective classroom manager deals with such misbehavior calmly, quickly, and without disrupting the flow of the lesson by using procedures such as

  o making *eye contact* with the student who is misbehaving;
  o reminding the student of the correct rule or procedure;
  o asking the student to repeat the correct rule; and
  o telling the student to stop the rule violation.

It is especially important that a teacher consistently enforces classroom rules and follows through with the consequences when students misbehave.

- **Plan ahead.** A teacher needs to have a very clear idea of what is to be taught and how it is to be taught. Therefore, planning is critical. Lessons should be planned and organized coherently before the class begins. Such planning allows a teacher to anticipate problems and any difficulties that students are likely to experience when the new material is introduced. Effective teachers often do the students' assignments beforehand so they can have a better idea of the task facing the student.

Beleaguered teachers comment on how problem students cause them such headaches. However, they quickly begin to equivocate when asked about how they monitor student behavior, or handle inappropriate behavior, or if they plan ahead. That is why it is imperative for teachers to check themselves periodically in order to notice areas where they can improve their classroom management and remain positive and proactive.

The Teacher Classroom Management Self-Check provides a teacher with a rating scale to analyze how well they are doing managing their own behavior. These mental prompts help teachers govern their behavior and act as a reminder to be proactive rather than reactive. The classroom management self-check consists of ten items to be rated by the teacher with three or more questions per item. For example, circle a (3) if you are doing this consistently; check a (2) if you do this but are somewhat inconsistent; and check a (1) if you are not doing this currently or struggling to implement. Blaming your students or making excuses for your behavior (making statements such as, "if only they had placed this child appropriately," or "he or she has ADD—that's why they are driving me crazy," or "kids today aren't like the old days," or "kids don't listen anyway") does nothing but lead to frustration and more behavior problems. This checklist provides you, the teacher, with an opportunity to analyze your own teaching behaviors and make adjustments. Identify a few items where you scored a (1) or a (2) and then decide how you'd like to tackle those items. Use the *checking myself box template* to begin to determine how you can make changes. A sample *checking myself box* is filled out below and a blank template is included at the end of the book.

TEACHER CLASSROOM MANAGEMENT CHECKLIST

When filling out the self-check, circle a (3) if you are doing this consistently; check a (2) if you do this but are somewhat inconsistent; and check a (1) if you are not doing this currently or struggling to implement.

1. Do you have a plan (and are willing to change it)—students need changes from hour to hour and from transition to transition?			
• Do you stick to your generic classroom management plan, yet remain sensitive to individual needs as new situations arise?	(1)	(2)	(3)
• Are the rules or expectations posted for you and your students to see?	(1)	(2)	(3)
• Do you continuously reinforce the classroom rules and expectations?	(1)	(2)	(3)
2. Do you anticipate problems (the "yellow light" always goes on before the "red light")? Students always send a signal ("yellow light") to let you know that a problem is brewing.			
• Do you anticipate the problem and remove it so behavior does not escalate?	(1)	(2)	(3)
• Do you have a clear classroom structure in place and a routine established?	(1)	(2)	(3)
• Do students know what is expected of them every day?	(1)	(2)	(3)
3. Do you communicate assertively?			
• Do you set clear limits—no gray areas?	(1)	(2)	(3)
• Do you say what you mean, mean what you say?	(1)	(2)	(3)
• Do you stay calm—no yelling, threatening, questioning, or arguing?	(1)	(2)	(3)
• Do you separate the act (behavior) from the actor (student)?	(1)	(2)	(3)
• Do you resist *giving up* or *giving in* for example, making statements like "I don't care" or "whatever?"	(1)	(2)	(3)
• Do you use a clear and calm approach?	(1)	(2)	(3)

(Continued)

(Continued)

	(1)	(2)	(3)
4. Do you ignore attention-getting behaviors whenever possible?			
• Students who misbehave often need attention and will dangle a hook and wait for you to take the bait—do you bite?	(1)	(2)	(3)
• Do you reward appropriate behavior continually throughout the day?	(1)	(2)	(3)
• Do you provide varied learning experiences so students can move around?	(1)	(2)	(3)
5. Do you take conflicts personally or do you stay calm?			
• Do you stay neutral and listen to both sides?	(1)	(2)	(3)
• Do you establish clear ground rules for communication?	(1)	(2)	(3)
• Do you have clear ground rules established for transitions?	(1)	(2)	(3)
• Do you have clear ground rules established for group work?	(1)	(2)	(3)
6. Do you offer positive consequences and encouragement on a continual basis (kids really, really respond to that)?			
• Do you have lots of positive consequences and are they creative?	(1)	(2)	(3)
• Are you enthusiastic and encouraging?	(1)	(2)	(3)
• Do you vary the delivery of positive consequences?	(1)	(2)	(3)
7. Do you handle negative consequences well?			
• Are you respectful of the child or student?	(1)	(2)	(3)
• Are your negative consequences related to the behavior or the *crime*?	(1)	(2)	(3)
• Are your negative consequences reasonable?	(1)	(2)	(3)
• Do you resist arguing or counseling and act calmly when applying negative consequences (counsel later)?	(1)	(2)	(3)
• Do you follow through while staying calm and neutral?	(1)	(2)	(3)
8. Do you take personal time?			
• Do you create and build a bridge and establish relationships with students?	(1)	(2)	(3)
• Are you genuinely interested in their lives?	(1)	(2)	(3)
• Have you created a true sense of belonging and trust in your classroom?	(1)	(2)	(3)
9. Do you have a system for evaluation?			
• Do you change as necessary to meet the needs of your students?	(1)	(2)	(3)
• Do you call on your colleagues for assistance, and to brainstorm options?	(1)	(2)	(3)
• Do you settle for anything but success?	(1)	(2)	(3)
10. Do you motivate your students?			
• Are your lessons well-planned out?	(1)	(2)	(3)
• Do you have a clear idea of what is to be taught and how it is to be taught?	(1)	(2)	(3)
• Do you provide an *obnoxious* amount of encouragement?	(1)	(2)	(3)
• Do you teach with joy and does that joy show through to your students?	(1)	(2)	(3)
• Do you have a sense of humor and use humor in your classroom?	(1)	(2)	(3)

Checking Myself Sample

Checking Myself Box

Checklist Item: # 5 (Don't take conflicts personally-stay calm)

Rating: I

Checklist Question: Do you establish clear ground rules for transitions?

Response and Action: I want to work on setting clear ground rules for transitions to reduce the noise, confusion, and behavior problems. I will make a list of simple ground rules and model them for my students. I will then reiterate the ground rules calmly if students are not complying with the established ground rules. By doing this, I will stop hearing myself saying expressions like "shhhh," "remember what I told you," "quit it," "you're going to get a check," and "that's a warning." After two weeks I will reflect and evaluate my response and, if satisfied, take on another review area I identified on the self-check.

Filling out the *Checking Myself Box* takes only a few moments but will pay off by spending less time managing student behavior. Make certain to review and incorporate some of the suggested ideas found in the book when filling out the response and action part of this management guide.

SCHOOL BEHAVIOR CHECKLIST

It is very important to have clear classroom expectations for individual and group behavior. Equally important are techniques that teachers can use to reinforce classroom expectations. The following *School Behavior Checklist* gives students an opportunity to become more self-reliant. Teaching students *how to learn* is half the battle for most teachers; however, it cannot be left to chance. First, model how to fill out the checklist by role-playing a student. In the role play show your students the correct way to fill out the checklist and then model the wrong way by putting a rating of *mastered* by every item. Then have the entire class fill out every item with you. Students can fill out the checklist individually if you feel comfortable with them doing so. Next, help students select an item from the checklist in each of the three designated areas (before, during and after class) and have them jot it down in the the *My Progress Goals Sheet.* You will again need to model this task for the students. Let the students know that change in behavior starts with awareness. After students become aware of their behavior they can then begin to take more responsibility for their actions. The *My Progress Goals* sheet helps students focus on key skills needed to be a successful student. Teachers are encouraged to develop and add items to the checklist as they see fit.

SCHOOL BEHAVIOR CHECKLIST

Student _____   Period _____   Date _____

Think about the past week in this class. For each school behavior, place a check in the box labeled *mastered*, *partially mastered*, or *need help with*.

Mastered	Partially Mastered	Need Help With	Before Class School Behaviors
			- Complete my homework
			- Arrive on time and enter class with a pleasant manner
			- Bring all materials to class (planner, notebook, pencils)
			- Get ready for learning/be prepared to listen (at my desk, group table, lab station)
			During Class School Behaviors
			- Follow classroom ground rules
			- Listen carefully to the teacher and my classmates
			- Participate in class activities
			- Participate in class discussions
			- Work cooperatively with my classmates
			- Respect classmates (no put downs, cliques, bullying, or exclusions of classmates)
			- Honor different points of view
			- Follow teacher directives
			- Ask for assistance
			- Move quickly to new activity or new class
			- Complete assigned work in class and turn it in
			- Write down assignments and important due dates in planner or notebook
			- Respect other students' privacy and property
			- Help and encourage other students
			- Keep workspace clean
			- Use and treat materials properly
			Cooperative Group Work
			- Transition to group work quietly and quickly
			- Complete my part of a group project on time
			- Be a good team member and hard worker
			After Class School Behavior:
			- Take materials home
			- Schedule a time to do my homework
			- Have a designated space to do my homework
			- Complete one homework assignment at a time
			- Arrange time to use home computer
			- Complete homework adequately
			- Collect materials and put in one spot before bed
			- Bring homework back to class

Source: Adapted with permission from *Success With the Difficult Learner*, Diana Browning Wright from presentation materials by Anita Archer and Mary Gleason, "Skills for Schools Success." Copyright © Diana Browning Wright.

School Behavior Progress Goals Sheet

Once students have completed the *School Behavior Checklist* by themselves or with the teacher's assistance, each student chooses one of the items from the list that was rated *partially mastered* or *needs help with*. The students discuss their chosen items with the teacher, write down their goals, and begin working on them right away. At the end of the first or second week, they indicate whether they accomplished their goals by circling *Yes*, or if the goal is still in progress, circling *In Progress*. A *Student Progress Goals Sheet* folder should be created and kept in the classroom for students to complete and then develop new goals. The teacher should schedule a time for this activity to review completed goals and discuss new goals. Students can also share their goals with other students whether they are working on similar goals or different ones. The *My Progress Goals Sheet* promotes students taking responsibility for their behavior and supports their working toward identified goals as is evidenced by the sample below (see My Progress Goals Template in Appendix 5).

My Progress Goals

BEFORE: (example) ***Arrive on time and enter class with a pleasant manner***

    First Week: Yes   In Progress

    Second Week: Yes   In Progress

WHEN IN CLASS: (example) ***Move quickly to a new activity or new class***

    First Week: Yes   In Progress

    Second Week: Yes   In Progress

AFTER CLASS: (example) ***Bring homework back to class.***

    First Week: Yes   In Progress

    Second Week: Yes   In Progress

The reward for accomplishing one, two, or all three goals is determined by the teacher. The student continues to work on additional goals. The classroom has to be highly structured and time needs to be allocated for these individualized, student–teacher interactions. Teaching school behaviors must be a priority equal to teaching math or language arts; if not, it will be an activity moored on the shoals of good intention.

CLASS MEETINGS

Class meetings are a great way for your students to gain a sense of belonging and greater involvement in the classroom. Class meetings take about 15 minutes and can be built into the curriculum (one or two times a week) or spontaneously convened, as the need arises. At the middle and high school level, the class meeting is usually conducted with everyone sitting in a circle facing each other, and at the elementary school level the children sit on the floor or carpet with chairs, desks, or tables pushed out of the way. The purpose for holding class meetings includes giving compliments, helping each other solve problems, and planning events. At the start of each meeting it is a good idea to post the agenda and then go over it with the students, at least with the first few meetings.

Meetings begin with compliments. The teacher or student leader picks someone to start the compliments and then goes around the circle until everyone has either *passed* or had an opportunity to compliment someone. Compliments should involve acknowledging others for their accomplishments and helpfulness. After compliments the agenda is covered. An agenda is posted somewhere in the classroom that is easily accessible to all students. When students have a problem they can write it down on the agenda (or just write their name). Using the agenda often allows a student a cooling-off period and the problem gets solved without needing a class meeting. The student can then choose to erase his or her name or leave it on the agenda.

Since students apply consequences for misbehavior during class meetings, they are taught the three R's of applying consequences: (1) Related to the transgression, (2) Respectful of the student, (3) Reasonable or "fits the crime." They learn to apply the three R's when deciding as a group appropriate consequences or solutions to problems. Here is an example of how the three R's might work. A student pushes another student in class. The consequence decided upon during the class meeting might be that the student who pushed his or her classmate stays in the classroom for recess for one day, and sincerely apologizes to the pushed student. The consequence is related, respectful, and reasonable.

During a class meeting, the teacher or student leader reads the first item on the agenda and checks with that student to see if it is still a problem. If it remains a problem and another student is involved, the person who wrote it on the agenda talks first. Then you might have the *accused* (other involved party) offer a solution, and the class can vote as to the acceptability of the solution. If a satisfactory solution is not reached in this manner then go around the circle and let classmates offer possible solutions. Suggestions should be written down and read over. Prior to a vote, the class decides on the best solution to the problem. Everyone's vote, including the teacher's vote, has equal weight. When the final vote is in, ask the wronged person if it solves the problem. The person can suggest a slight modification to the solution; however, he or she cannot at this point argue for a solution change. The modification is accepted via an "all in favor" vote (raise your hand), or an "all against" vote (raise your hand). In essence, the majority rules in a *three R's* case. If a consequence is to be applied, students utilize the three R's. The consequence can be a suggestion by an individual student or group of students. Once that particular issue is completed, move on to the next item on the agenda, Remember to stick with the 15 minute time frame (See Classroom Meeting Agenda Template below).

There are some very important teacher skills that go along with conducting successful class meetings. Teachers should model appropriate compliments and appropriate courtesy statements such as *please, thank you,* and *you are welcome.* Students should be given the chance to practice coming up with consequences that fit the three R's; role-playing is often successful. Teachers should practice using open-ended questions to encourage students to develop their own ideas, for example, "What are a few reasons you can think of for your actions?" The teacher must be willing to take ownership of his or her part in any problem and be as nonjudgmental as possible so that the students know they can discuss subjects with impunity. Agenda items should not be censored. Finally, it is important to find the positive intent behind every behavior. Many of these class meeting suggestions have been adapted with permission from a *Positive Behavior Intervention Workshop* that was conducted by Diana Browning Wright.

CLASSROOM MEETING AGENDA TEMPLATE

AGENDA ITEM # 1

Is it still a problem?   YES   NO

If the answer is yes, proceed to accuser's solution.

Is the accuser's solution accepted?   YES   NO

If the answer is no, proceed to the classmate's solution.

Classmate's suggested solutions:

1. _____
_____
_____
_____
_____

2. _____
_____
_____
_____
_____

3. _____
_____
_____
_____
_____

Read over possible solutions.

Class votes on best solution.

Ask if the solution solves the problem. YES   MODIFY

If the answer is to modify, ask the student to suggest a slight modification.

Modification accepted by classmates via hand vote—all in favor raise your hand—all against raise your hand.

Three R's consequences applied—*Related, Respectful, and Reasonable.*

Classroom meetings require clarifying the process, understanding terms, and learning sophisticated problem solving. Teachers who use classroom meetings must be self-assured and their teaching style should incorporate a student-centered methodology. Classroom meetings cannot be an afterthought or just a good idea to try out; they must be planned, monitored, and evaluated for optimum success.

COOPERATIVE/COLLABORATIVE LEARNING

The timeworn adage says *Prevention is worth a pound of cure*. This is true for medicine as well as for many walks of life. When teachers advocate and promote opportunities for students to negotiate and cooperate then behavior problems seem to dissipate. By solving problems and learning through cooperation and negotiation, students definitely feel more competent, capable, and empowered. What characteristics embody cooperation and negotiation and how are those defining features manifested in a classroom?

Cooperative learning theory, as developed by Roger and David Johnson (1991), provides multiple opportunities for students to exercise teamwork, to solve problems together, to maximize their strengths as learners, and to produce a product that is often greater than the sum of its parts. Students who participate in cooperative groups (have delegated roles and duties when working on assignments) learn to become interdependent and to realize that each and every member of the group makes an important contribution to the group. Cooperative or collaborative learning requires that teachers conscientiously create cooperative groups to maximize learning. The teacher, either directly or indirectly, creates guidelines for behavior, assigns roles, gives time limits for completion, and then guides the learning. Cooperative groups demand that consequences are established to ensure that students stay on task, learn from one another, show empathy for other students, and produce a product that they are proud of as a group. Through cooperation, students learn to care for one another, listen attentively to each other, and most importantly, take responsibility for their role in the group. A cooperative group that is "humming" along values each member's contribution and does not allow one student to take over or another student to *hitchhike* along just for the ride. Every moment in a cooperative group must be accounted for with active student engagement that is both prized and encouraged by the teacher. If that is not the case, then it is just group work in the classroom, which often lacks purpose.

Since cooperative learning has been around for several decades, some form of group work can be seen taking place in public school classrooms. As I mentioned, most group work does not employ the key ingredients essential in cooperative learning: interdependency, role identification, team results, democracy within disagreement, active attention and communication, nonjudgmental response, deadline adherence, and teacher recognition and validation. Empowering students with decision making and problem solving through cooperative learning reduces *managing* behavior. When students feel empowered and valued by teachers, they reciprocate, maintaining a sense of classroom decorum.

Let's take a look at how a cooperative group might operate in a public school classroom.

What Cooperative Learning Looks Like:

- The teacher establishes the ground rules or norms for working in cooperative learning groups, for example, when a student offers an opinion, reserve judgment and avoid comments such as "that's dumb" or "that won't work." All opinions and thoughts no matter how "wonky" or crazy must be considered.

- The transition from large group activity to a small group is clearly communicated and a time of between 1 and 2 minutes is designated for the change. Once assembled in their small cooperative groups, students must be in a ready-to-learn position—sitting up and waiting for instructions from the teacher.

- Once in the cooperative groups, identified roles are established for all members. For instance, in a group of five students, one student might be the scribe, another the timekeeper, another a gatekeeper (ensures that everyone's thoughts and opinions are honored), another an encourager, and lastly a runner who gathers materials for the group.

- This type of learning requires an activity that is content driven and associated with the state standards, where students use fact-finding, analytical, evaluation, or synthesizing skills, and develop some form of product such as a report, demonstration or project. The process and product must have a time-frame for completion.

- The teacher employs active student-engagement strategies to promote peer interaction, for example, *pair share* which is where students pair up in the group and think about the topic, and then one person is designated to share their thoughts with the rest of the group. Use a *KWL Chart*, (**K**—what I know, **W**—what I want to know, **L**—what I learned) for members of the cooperative group to fill in.

- Assessment is an important aspect of cooperative learning. Each member is responsible for doing his or her part and must be given some acknowledgment for his or her contribution. Usually a summative evaluation or a grade is given for the project as a whole and students are also given individual grades. Along the way, teachers using formative assessment to check for understanding provide students with valuable information to help them cooperate and complete the prescribed assignment.

- The end product can be displayed or discussed with the entire class. The teacher can assign grades as indicated based on the outlined objectives for the assignment.

Ms. Lincoln's eighth-grade history lesson is on democracy and the students are assembled in their cooperative groups with identified roles. The group size of six has one scribe/notetaker, encourager, timekeeper, gatekeeper, runner, and a computer wizard. The computer wizard can access a computer in the class or use a laptop if one is available for student use. The teacher gives the students the first of two activities related to understanding democracy. For activity one, the teacher asks students to define democracy. She uses a *Whip Around Strategy* where each student in the group has to quickly share his or her definition of democracy. The teacher then gives the students about 20 seconds of thinking time to generate ideas. She tells the student with the longest hair to start and then proceeds clockwise around the group. She gives them one minute. If they end before the minute is up, she instructs them to keep going around or to add to their definition. She also tells students they can pass if they have a mental block, but really encourages them to take a stab at the definition. The students all chuckle when they share their definitions and complete the task seemingly amazed at the variety of definitions presented for democracy.

Next, the teacher gives the students 5 minutes to complete the task of writing all of the definitions down on a flip chart. After that, she asks the *runners* to get a sheet of the flip chart and bring it to their respective groups. The *scribe* writes down the question, "How do you define democracy?" He then proceeds to write down all of the group members' definitions. The *gatekeeper* ensures that all definitions are represented appropriately while the *encourager* gives high fives to various group members. The *timekeeper* signals timed intervals with a beeping noise. The *computer wizard* looks up various definitions to assess the accuracy of the group members' definitions. The teacher at the 2½ minute mark tells the students to consolidate their definitions, including anything they learned from the computer, into one group definition that all can agree upon. At that moment, she tells the timekeepers to add 2 additonal minutes. Everyone is actively engaged in the task and the teacher acts as a guide on the side. At the end, the timekeeper blurts out his final beep and then the scribe must share the group's definition while group members can add comments. The teacher writes down the groups' definitions on the board.

The next activity is yet another question, "Why would people risk their lives for democracy?" Here the teacher uses a *collective brainstorming strategy* so that students can see that there are many ways to answer this compelling question. The scribe writes down or graphically represents all contributions. The roles remain the same. The gatekeeper needs to spring into action to ensure that all contributions are noted, and the encourager must be on his or her toes to keep each student active and engaged. The students are then asked to assemble their *brainstorms* into categories, add any new ideas, or elaborate on what is already written. The timekeeper (an active contributor) signals an end to the process. The encourager is asked to share their answers.

Cooperative learning, when implemented appropriately, promotes equality in a classroom filled with diverse learners. Students learn from each other, solve problems together, rely on one another, and stay actively engaged in learning. Effective cooperative learning hinges on teachers regularly incorporating this method into their classroom structure. A wonderful by-product of well-managed cooperative learning is a reduction in behavioral problems. When students feel valued and included, learning is fun.

CONFLICT RESOLUTION

Conflict between peers and teachers, especially at the secondary level, is to be expected. Unfortunately, conflict is often perceived as negative and to be avoided at all costs. Teaching students and teachers how to handle conflict can be instructive and empowering. Creating some sort of an agreement between parties (in this case, students) that differ requires a clear an identified process that teachers can put into practice on a regular basis. Restoring broken communication in a relationship takes practice and requires skills such as active listening, empathizing, and rephrasing so that students and teachers alike can come to a resolution that seems fair and equitable. Conflict resolution encourages both parties to repair their relationship and, in the best-case scenario, to regenerate a new relationship based on mutual understanding. A wonderful book by Roger Fisher and William Ury, *Getting to Yes: Negotiating Agreement Without Giving In*, discusses the importance of *principled negotiation*, a process where one separates the person from the problem and insists on using available objective criteria. The following conflict resolution approach uses tenets of principled negotiation to help students resolve conflicts themselves.

Conflict Styles: Aggressive, Passive, Problem-Solving

Generally, people tend to be *aggressive* or attacking when presented with a conflict situation, or *passive* and denying that the conflict exists. The aggressor is usually determined to be right and to prove the other person wrong. The passive person often doesn't want to deal with the conflict at all. These two styles, though unsuccessful, are used in most conflict interactions. When individuals adopt an aggressive or passive style of behavior toward conflict, it creates a *win–loss* situation ensuring that the conflict will not be resolved in an amicable manner and most likely will reoccur. A third style, *problem solving*, turns conflict into a *win–win* situation.

If conflict is viewed as an opportunity to learn and grow from the experience, then a degree of harmony will be restored with both parties gaining an enhanced understanding of one another's differing points of view. Moreover, it increases the likelihood that communication between both parties improves, fostering acceptance and tolerance for diversity of opinion. As a result, both parties are more prone to develop a verbal or written agreement of how to interact with one another in the near future thus laying the groundwork for long-lasting positive interactions. However, to restore harmony between parties does not happen without some sort of problem-solving model with clearly articulated steps and agreements and an investment in honest and open communication.

Communication

Communication comes from the Latin word *communicare*, or to care about what we say and about how others see the world. Communication must include a meaningful exchange of perceptions between the sender and the receiver. When two people are able to communicate clearly—to understand, to be heard, and to be understood—then there really is no problem in communication at all. Unfortunately, poor communication causes most conflict. On the other hand, clear communication is necessary for effective problem solving and conflict resolution.

As educators we must also be aware that students come from different cultures, and different ethnic, linguistic, and family backgrounds. Students have diverse personal experiences, aspirations, and expectations. Our most important role as educators then becomes one of understanding and incorporating these unique differences into our instruction. We must also be keenly aware that these differences potentially can become conflict *hot buttons*. If teachers appreciate student diversity, most conflicts can be averted or handled responsibly by establishing opportunities for students to engage in meaningful dialogue, through cooperative groups, classroom meetings, student councils, service learning projects, and social skills training. Students need to feel that their opinions are valued and that what they say is taken seriously.

Student–Teacher Conflict Resolution

Sometimes conflicts arise between teachers and students. It is not out of the ordinary for a student to "rub a teacher the wrong way," thus creating fertile ground for conflict. To resolve conflicts and restore harmony, teachers must understand (though it may be difficult) that they are the more mature individual guiding the less mature student. The following seven-step approach is very beneficial to helping resolve conflicts and to restoring harmony between teachers and students.

(1) Define the problem as clearly as possible.

(2) Share your feelings using this sentence starter: I feel _____ about _____ because _____ therefore_____. Keep it short and to the point without blaming each other.

(3) Generate some ideas about how you might solve the problem.

(4) Discuss the pros and cons of your solution and then narrow it down to what appears to be a workable solution.

(5) Create an action plan. Specify the exact time the plan will begin and how you will assess its effectiveness. Both the teacher and the student should sign the plan.

(6) After one week, review the plan on a specific scheduled day. If the plan needs to be modified, do so at that time. Decide on another review date.

(7) If the conflict is resolved and harmony is restored, shake hands and acknowledge one another.

Conflict Resolution With Difficult Students

As indicated earlier, most conflict can be averted between students and teachers if positive interaction and openness prevail in interpersonal communication. However, when students for one reason or another adopt an aggressive or passive conflict resolution style, they can present the teacher with challenges that could inadvertently push them into a *fight or flight* response pattern. To deal effectively with difficult students follow these simple negotiation rules:

- Take what the student is saying seriously.
- Stay calm and focused.
- Maintain eye contact.
- Acknowledge feelings by using "I" statements such as, "I hear what you are saying," "I have felt that way as well," "It hurts my feelings when you talk that way," "I feel _____ about _____ because _____ therefore _____."
- Don't take things personally.
- Stay mature and don't *fight or flee*.
- Redirect statements that are off topic or not related to the issue at hand.
- Paraphrase and summarize to ensure that the student feels as if they are being heard.
- Drive for a workable solution.
- Clarify a timeline, "I have about 5 minutes before I have yard duty. If you need more time you can see me at 12:35 p.m. for 10 minutes."
- Walk away if the student is unreasonable, uses foul language, or stops talking. Let the student know why you are walking away and give the student an option to talk now in a reasonable manner or at another convenient time. If it is a school infraction indicate the consequence for the student's behavior. If it is a classroom infraction apply appropriate negative consequences.

Conflict Resolution—Student to Student:

The seven steps outlined above don't just work for difficult students but work equally as well for all students. A mediator (often a student, conflict resolution coordinator, peer counselor, or the teacher) remains neutral and guides the students through the seven steps. According to Johns and Carr (1995) this process promotes dispute settlements through active listening, problem analyzing, and cooperative decision making (see Conflict Resolution Form, Appendix 6).

A Conflict Resolution Coordinator might use the following steps:

- "Hi my name is _____ and I'm a Conflict Resolution Coordinator. I know this is a long title, but all it means is that I am here to listen to you and to understand where things might have gone wrong in the communication so that you can resolve your differences and come to some honorable agreement." (This wording can vary at the high school level but is appropriate at the elementary and junior high school level).
- "Do you want to solve the problem with us?"
- If yes, move to a different area to talk.
- "Will you agree to 4 rules?

  do not interrupt;
  no name calling or put-downs are allowed;
  try to be as honest as you can; and
  agree to solve the problem."

Defining the Problem

- "Who will talk first?"
- Ask person #1, "What happened?" *Restate.*
- Ask person #1, "How do you feel? Why?"
- Ask person #2, "What happened?" *Restate.*
- Ask person #2, "How do you feel? Why?"

Finding Solutions

- Ask person #1, "What can you do to resolve your part of the problem?"
- Ask person #2, "Do you agree?"
- Ask person #2, "What can you do to resolve your part of the problem?"
- Ask person #1, "Do you agree?"
- Ask each disputant, "What could you do differently if this problem happens again?"
- Ask them both, "Is the problem solved?"
- Ask disputants, "Please tell your friends that the conflict has been solved to prevent rumors from spreading."
- Repeat to both students, "Congratulations on your hard work solving this dispute."
- Fill out the conflict resolution coordinator report form.

Source: "Conflict Resolution—Student-to-Student," and "A Conflict Resolution Counselor might use the following steps" have been adapted from *Classroom Conflict Resolution Training for Elementary Schools,* Community Boards, San Francisco, CA. All rights reserved. For more information, visit www .communityboards.org.

Conflict Resolution Coordinator Report Form

Conflict Resolution Coordinator(s) _____

Date _____

Who had the conflict? _____

What kind of conflict?

    ❏ Argument   ❏ Fight   ❏ Rumor   ❏ Other

How did you find out about it?

    ❏ Student   ❏ Yard Duty Supervisor   ❏ Teacher

    ❏ Aide   ❏ Counselor   ❏ Yourself

What was the conflict about? _____

Was the conflict resolved? _____ Yes _____ No

Resolution:

Student #1 agrees to	Student # 2 agrees to

Along with ways to handle individual conflict, the school should have a system in place for schoolwide discipline. A schoolwide discipline plan puts safety first and communicates to staff, students, and parents that the students who have persistent or egregious behavior will be dealt with in a direct, effective, and orderly manner. A *School Discipline Report Form* is included in Appendix 8 and addresses behaviors that warrant intervention by teachers, administration, and counselors.

CLASSROOM MANAGER ROLES

(Pre-K through Junior High School Students)

Most students, whether in a regular classroom or in a special education setting, want to feel capable, competent, and helpful. Classroom managers perform jobs that help the classroom run smoothly while at the same time providing students with valuable leadership opportunities. Manager positions help to free up teacher time while at the same time giving students a sense of self-worth, and a sense of ownership and responsibility to the classroom. Classroom managers' job descriptions, responsibilities, and expectations can be varied or adjusted to meet each individual teacher's needs and the requirements of the students and the school. The number of jobs assigned to the students can also be adapted. It is often a good idea to begin the school year with a few positions in place, and then create or add new jobs as the school year progresses. Manager jobs may be determined in conjunction with input from the students or created as needed by the teacher. The following classroom manager roles are by no means an exhaustive list. They were developed to give you a few ideas that you might find useful, interesting, and possibly a good fit for your particular classroom setting and style of teaching.

Wearing Different Hats—For each manager role, a hat is used to designate each job. For younger students, in addition to assuming the responsibility, just getting to wear the hat for a while can act as an incentive.

- **Chef's Hat**—Can help with setting the table, passing out snacks, and any other food-related activities.
- **Construction Helmet**—Maintenance jobs, for example, turning lights on and off, making certain trash is in the trash can, and sweeping up.
- **Gardener's Hat**—Waters the plants.
- **Railroad Hat**—Line leader, stands in front of the line for other students to follow. Eventually is able to signal students to line up.
- **Postal Hat**—Delivers notes to office or other teachers. Passes out notices and school handouts.
- **Sports Cap**—In charge of playground equipment, recreation materials, toys, etc.

Setup Suggestions: Place hats on a long hat rack with photos of the students underneath each hat, so each child knows which hat to wear.

Agenda Manager—Teacher will give the student the daily agenda and student writes it on the board everyday.

Attendance Manager—Takes attendance folder to office every morning. Sometimes takes other notes or fund-raiser paperwork to the office usually at the same time as taking the attendance folder. They may also take the lunch count to the cafeteria when necessary. Depending on the ability level of the students and school regulations, this duty may also include marking absences and tardies on the attendance roster before taking it to the office (after being checked by the teacher).

Board Manager—Cleans the boards every day.

Books Manager—Distributes and reshelves textbooks upon teacher's request. Picks up stray books and shelves them at the end of the day.

Brainstorm Manager—Dramatizes weekly concepts, brainstorms related issues and ideas from real-world experiences to connect with the material of the week, and writes individually or with other students an essay, poem, or rap related to what was learned that week.

Cafeteria Manager—Ensures that everyone has lunch. Helps monitor clean-up.

Calendar Manager—Puts current date on the calendar every day. Ensures that holidays and days off are recorded. This job can also include indicating the weather on the weather chart. In kindergarten and primary grades, this manager can determine which day is today, tomorrow, yesterday, or other special days.

Captain Vocabulary—Monitors and supports instruction and with the help of the teacher introduces a list of new words to the class, goes over the words with students in the class, gives weekly spelling test or vocabulary check, and assists with election of the captain vocabulary for the next week.

Center Director—Monitors the class centers and answers any questions during center time. They also let the teacher know when the centers need more materials.

Clean-up Manager— After activities, supervises clean-up and determines when it has been done correctly. Assigns others to take a trash can around the room, put away supplies, or whatever else needs to be done. The manager checks the inside and outside of class desks to determine if clean and neat (about once a week).

Current Affairs Manager—Reports to the class any new information. He or she also passes out any newsletters from the school and reads them to the class. They can also report on any issue in the news that is important.

Desks & Chairs Manager—Rearranges desks and chairs when required, places furniture in assigned spaces at the end of the day, and puts up chairs at the end of the day.

Doors & Lights Manager—Turns out lights and shuts door after last person is out, and makes certain that the door is locked. In charge of lights and curtains when video is being shown or when there is a need for a darkened room.

Dr. Book—Reviews and selects a book from an approved list of books prepared by the teacher, introduces the theme of the book, gives a brief summary of the book at the end of the week, and holds discussions on the book in class. This job is done by Dr. Book and a committee.

Dr. Math—Introduces new concepts to the class, gives examples for each concept, announces homework assignments, collects homework assignments, answers questions from class with assistance from teacher, goes over most common errors found in the assignments, explains the proper steps to avoid repeating the same mistakes again, and works with fellow peers in a group or an individual basis.

Equipment Manager—Passes out all the PE and recess equipment. They have a sign-up list and are responsible for equipment returns.

Errands & Notes Manager—Runs errands, for example gets books from the library, takes notes to another teacher or office, escorts a student to the office for illness, injury, or other issue, passes out notes distributed by the office, and passes out book-club order forms.

File Clerk—Files corrected papers in students' files.

First Aid Manager—Gets first aid kit for teacher and delivers notes to nurse's office.

Floor Manager—Picks up pencils, papers, trash, etc. at teacher's request and during the end of the day's clean-up period.

Gatekeeper—Manages conflicts in the classroom. When students need to vent and resolve conflicts, the gatekeeper is in charge.

Homework Manager— First thing in the morning, checks to see if all students have completed the homework assignments due that day. Sometimes collects homework assignments and alphabetizes them. Sometimes the manager may even correct or check off homework assignments depending upon the assignment.

Journal Topic Manager—Writes the journal topic on the board every morning.

Library Manager—Ensures that all library books are neat and returned in order.

Line Leaders—Leads the students in from outside and vice versa. Leads the line to other activities. Teachers can elect to have one person in the front, the other in the back. Students can work out their own systems for determining which manager is in front and who is in back. Responsible to see that others maintain appropriate behavior, for example, that they stay in line, don't run, and don't stop for a drink.

Lunch Tickets Manager—At a predetermined time, goes to the cafeteria to pick up lunch tickets, returns to class, passes out lunch tickets, and gives the lunch ticket envelope to the line leader.

Maintenance Crew—Keeps the classroom clean. These students also excuse the students for recess and lunch when their designated areas are deemed clean.

Month Committee—Summarizes learned materials dramatizing concepts together for the class, prepares and organizes one-hour lunch fun or an afternoon activity that relates to all the knowledge and information learned for the month.

Paper & Supplies Manager—Passes out necessary paper and supplies for classroom work, for example, paper for spelling tests, art supplies, rulers, worksheets, workbooks, and other books.

Pencils Manager—Collects and sharpens pencils at the end of the day.

Pet Manager—Feeds class pets every day or every other day. This student may also be in charge of taking the class pet outside of its cage (home) and monitoring other student's time with the pet. This student can also be in charge of the list of students who get to take the pet home for the weekend. This job is done for one week.

Phone Manager—Answers the intercom or phone and relays any message to the teacher.

Plant Manager—Checks plants to see if they need water and waters them when needed. This student keeps a chart of how much water the plants receive every week.

Positive Bird—Makes certain that every student in the class hears a positive statement about himself or herself every day. This can be a committee of students.

Recycling Managers—Recycles all papers and cans into the proper bins everyday. They are provided with plastic gloves, because sometimes they will have to take things out of the trash cans. This job usually involves two students.

Reminder Manager—Reminds others, including and especially the teacher, if someone forgets something, for example if the teacher says a certain activity will happen at a certain time, the reminder manager lets the teacher know the time and/or activity that needs to begin. Reminding is done according to the preestablished class rules so as not to be disruptive.

Snack Manager—Washes hands and passes out snack. Also responsible for making certain that they know how many of the snack (i.e., crackers) each student can have.

Spell Check Managers—Helps the teacher out if she or he spells a word wrong or needs help. They can also help their classmates with any spelling problems. They are provided with a small, spelling dictionary.

Substitute Manager—Greets guests and/or substitute teachers. Provides visitors with the information they need. This student needs instruction prior to performing this job.

Table Manager—Oversees the work done at his or her table. May pass out materials and help others work on assignments when appropriate or required.

Technology Manager—Helps out any student on the computer and is in charge of the sign-up sheet. Monitors that computers are turned off correctly after class and programs are in place. Assists in providing other technology as needed. This job requires that the student have an understanding of the computer.

Time Keeper—Helps keep track of activities that should only take a certain amount of time, such as timed tests, art projects, or group discussions.

Xerox Manager—Takes the things that need to be copied to the office. The student will be trained on how to use the copy machine and is trusted not to misuse it.

PART II

Activities to Promote Positive Classroom and Student Behavior

The menu of activities in Part II further reinforces the general principles articulated in Part I. The listed activities are teacher-friendly, applicable to real-world classrooms, and quick and easy to implement. Teachers can peruse the activities in this section until they hit upon one that strikes their fancy, mark it with a placeholder, and then continue reading through the rest of the activities. Teachers can and should feel free to modify any of the activities to fit their individual style of teaching. In many ways, the activities are intended to function like a bank of ideas. You may notice when thumbing through the activities that you can withdraw some of these very ideas and incorporate them into your current classroom management system. This validation of your proactive approach to classroom management and student empowerment will hopefully give you cause to celebrate. The hope is that you notice a few new activities that pique your interest and that you want to try out in your respective classrooms.

A menu of behavior management activities, though helpful, only goes so far. One must keep in mind that the purpose of a behavior management approach or system is to empower students to take more responsibility for their individual, small group, and whole-class behavior. Changing any of the activities included in this section or adding new activities to fit the behavioral challenges of your students is encouraged. Consider this option. Ask a group of students to look over the activities and suggest a few to you that they think would really be good to implement in the classroom. When students select a behavior approach they think will work, they tend to comply with its requirements. When they choose the behavioral method, you no longer need to remind, cajole, threaten, beg, or counsel students to behave. Why? Because students have selected and now own the very methodology that will contain their behavior and that act, in and of itself, empowers both the students and the teacher.

Students often comment about teachers who seem to have a clear structure in place. They usually state, "That teacher has his or her act together; we know how to behave in so and so's class." "Our teacher has rules and doesn't let us get away with things." Good classroom behavior management skills create the context for an empowering classroom environment. However, it must be noted that many teachers do not have an organized classroom management system in place or use activities to empower student behavior. Teachers still "wing it" with the belief that things will work out and that children will comply and respond to an authority figure. When the students do not comply, the teacher then complains about children not paying attention, fidgeting, talking, pinching, poking, blurting, whispering, and falling out of their chairs. A better choice would be for the teacher to use the IeAM system and other empowering options mentioned in this book. The menu of activities included in this section gives teachers a few ideas and useful tools to help with classroom management but are not a replacement for the daily vigilance necessary to create a proactive and positive learning environment identified in Part I of this book.

"2:45 P.M.–3:00 P.M." STORE

Audience: Elementary.

Objective: To reinforce positive interactions in the classroom and encourage diligent work habits.

Materials: Tickets and Tokens. Reward small prizes such as school supplies, trading cards, stickers, or small toys.

Description: Tickets are handed out to students for exhibiting positive behavior.

Use: Specific classroom implementation to be completed by the selecting teacher.

When: To be used during class time.

Where: Use this activity anywhere on the school campus where instruction is being given.

How: Tickets are given out by classroom staff whenever they notice and want to reinforce particularly positive or effortful behavior. Tickets are also used, when one student is misbehaving, to reinforce other students to stay focused and remain in control. Students collect tickets in containers and total their tickets at the end of the day. Tickets are used as currency to purchase special activities, privileges, or prizes. Students also start each day being awarded a certain number of tickets according to their level (see Bravo Point System in this chapter).

> PINK   20 tickets
>
> ORANGE 10 tickets
>
> GREEN   5 tickets
>
> RED   1 ticket

Once a week the students have the opportunity to spend their tickets when the class "store" is open. The store stocks items that range in price from just a few tickets to hundreds of tickets. Students spend their tickets weekly or save all or some of their tickets toward the purchase of an expensive item. Students can make suggestions about items they would like the store to stock and negotiate a reasonable price with staff. Each student records his or her daily ticket total in a ticket register similar to the checking account registers used to record deposits and withdrawals. Students use their ticket registers to record daily deposits, maintain a balance, and record withdrawals when purchases are made from the classroom store.

ACCOMPLISHMENT JOURNAL

Audience: Any grade level (for nonwriters a tape recorder can be used).

Objective: To promote and encourage positive attention and self-esteem.

Materials: Writing journals, pencils, pens, and colored pencils.

Description: Students list, write or illustrate specific accomplishments they have achieved. The accomplishments can pertain to any aspect of their lives—academic, social, or familial. Each page is always dated.

Use: Specific classroom implementation to be completed by the selecting teacher.

When: Use during class time. This can be an impromptu activity by the students when they first arrive in the morning or after recess. This is an activity that should be prompted by the teacher to remind students to focus on their successes.

Where: In the classroom, the accomplishment journals are kept in a brightly decorated basket in the writer's workshop area.

How: At the beginning of the school year, the teacher passes out the journals and shows the colorful accomplishment's basket. The teacher then talks about the importance of remembering the good things everyone does throughout the day, week, and year. Periodically, the teacher tells students, "That's something to put in your accomplishment journal!" The teacher may want to keep his or her own accomplishment journal so that the teacher can also say, "I'm going to put this in my accomplishment journal." The students may share the journal with anyone they choose, but it is never to be opened by anyone other than the student!

Example: For example, a student who typically has sportsmanship issues but plays at the ball wall without any negative comments and does not get upset during the entire recess could come in from recess and write or illustrate the positive event.

ACHIEVEMENT CHART

Audience: Junior high school.

Objective: To encourage assignment completion.

Materials: Pencils, individual grids or charts, list of achievements/goals, computer, and computer games.

Description: When a student finishes an assignment or goal, a check is earned on his or her grid for the day—four checks = 5 minutes on the computer; this time can be accumulated. Friday is a good day to be on the computer for their earned time.

Use: Specific classroom implementation to be completed by the selecting teacher.

When: All day, inside and outside the classroom.

Where: Use anywhere on campus, even at home if coordinated with parent or guardian.

How: Compile a list of objectives (may be adapted or altered). Line this list up with a grid (see example) and check off all accomplishments. Four checks = 5 minutes on computer. This is also a great way to see what is missing in the daily routine (by the blank spaces), in order to concentrate on those areas. Make certain that you establish how many points can be given per day and per week. Grids can be stapled on top of each other, weekly.

Objectives	Daily pts.	Mon.	Tues.	Wed.	Thurs.	Fri.	Total weekly pts. possible	Total weekly pts. given
Finishes math assignment								
Hands to himself or herself								
Turns in homework								
Stays in seat during reading								
						Total pts.		

ACHIEVING THE SPIRIT OF ACADEMIC EXCELLENCE

Audience: Upper elementary to high school.

Objective: To encourage cooperative behavior and positive self-esteem.

Materials: None except for the students themselves, their efforts, brains, attitudes, and cooperation.

Description: To develop the self-esteem of each individual student in the classroom. The goal is to build a student's *can-do* attitude. This activity also promotes an attitude between students of encouragement and teamwork. It teaches good morals, a sense of fairness, and supports the spirit of learning. The approach discourages disruption in the classroom and encourages more interest from all students once they know that they each have an opportunity to take charge of the classroom. It also helps develop a professional, academic relationship between the teacher and the student. Moreover, the student feels valued and appreciated whether he or she is a high-level or a low-level achiever.

Use: Specific classroom implementation to be completed by the selecting teacher.

When: Every week.

Where: In the classroom.

How: Select a different student each week to experience an academic leadership role, giving each student throughout the school year an opportunity. Once the student is selected, the teacher identifies the tasks associated with the leadership role for that particular week. Provide a checklist of duties to the student, and the student must check those off at the end of the day. The students can keep the checklist on their desks or a copy can be kept in a file on the teacher's desk. On a daily basis, the teacher confers with the student and reviews the checklist, encouraging conversation and feedback while at the same time providing opportunities for changes to be considered. If the student leader provides peer tutoring, then a comment at the bottom of the checklist is warranted. At the end of the week the student leader shares with the entire class his or her impressions and the lessons learned from the experience.

THE ADVENTURES OF "REGIE"

Audience: Elementary.

Objective: To encourage homework completion.

Materials: Any stuffed animal (the teacher can name it whatever he or she wants), a journal book, popsicle sticks (one for each child), and a carry bag for your pet (a small backpack, etc.).

Description: Regie is the classroom pet, and every week one child is randomly picked to take Regie home for the week. A child's name is put in the drawing only by completing the weekly homework assignments.

Use: Specific classroom implementation to be completed by the selecting teacher.

When: This activity is for classroom time.

Where: This selected activity is for use in the classroom.

How: Put all of the student names on individual popsicle sticks. Every week that homework is assigned and a student returns his or her homework on time, that child's popsicle stick is placed in a jar for the drawing determining who gets to take Regie home for the week. The winning child then takes Regie home for the week and has to write about an adventure that he or she experienced together. The adventure can either be fact or fiction. For young children, the parents help their child write the adventure. Then when Regie returns to the classroom, that child shares the adventure story with the class. The child also gets to pick the next person to take Regie home, with the condition that Regie can only visit a child's home once every two weeks. That way every child gets a turn to take Regie home and to write an adventure story of their own!

ALL SMILES

Audience:	Elementary.
Objective:	To encourage students to set goals and work toward those goals.
Materials:	Index cards, smiley-face stickers, pocket chart, monthly calendar, special activity, or prize.
Description:	Students earn a class prize for appropriate behavior. Students set a daily goal and an "ultimate" goal.
Use:	Specific classroom implementation to be completed by the selecting teacher.
When:	Throughout the day.
Where:	In the classroom.
How:	Put each student's name on an individual index card. The student then decorates the card with smiley-face stickers. At the beginning of the day, students' cards are placed in a pocket chart (or on desk) with smiley-faces facing forward and upright. The objective is to keep the student's smiley faces upright and facing forward by making responsible choices. The students and teacher set behavioral criteria for students keeping their smiley faces facing forward. These could include individual behavioral or academic goals in accordance with IEPs. The teacher and students agree on a prize to work for, a daily class goal, and an "ultimate" goal.
Example:	Behavioral objective: Students must follow teacher directions upon the first request. Daily goal: 98 percent of the smiley faces must be facing forward at the end of the day. Ultimate goal: 17 smiley faces on the calendar equals a class party.

1. If a student does not act responsibly, the teacher restates the behavioral goal *specifically* and *calmly* and asks the student to turn his or her card upside down as a visual reminder to get back on track.

2. The student has a chance to turn the card upright if he or she stops the misbehavior within a specific amount of time. If the child complies in the time frame, the teacher praises the student and asks the student to return the card to the upright position.

3. If the student continues the misbehavior, the teacher explains that the card must be turned over so that the smiley face is no longer showing.

At the end of the day, if the students reach the daily goal, then the teacher places a smiley face on the calendar for that day. Once the class reaches the ultimate goal, they receive the predetermined prize.

Variation: The teacher can turn the card or ask the child to turn the card depending on which is less disruptive.

Important: In order for this activity to be successful, the teacher must be consistent with the reward system, respond quickly and calmly during the initial misbehavior, and look for and acknowledge appropriate behaviors.

ASSIGNMENT JAR

Audience: Junior high school special education setting (can be adapted for general education, upper elementary, and junior high school).

Objective: To encourage students to complete assignments.

Materials: A jar, small slips of paper, and a pen.

Description: Students earn a slip of paper for each assignment completed. Every six to nine weeks, in tandem with the grading periods, a slip of paper is drawn from the jar and redeemed for a free lunch valued at up to $5.00.

Use: Specific classroom implementation to be completed by the selecting teacher.

When: Slips are deposited as assignments are corrected.

Where: In the classroom.

How: The teacher or aide writes the student's name on a slip of paper, folds it, and places it in the jar, as the student's assignments are corrected and deemed complete. There is one jar for each of the 10 students. At the end of each six to nine week grading period, the names are mixed well and one is drawn from the jar. That student is treated by the teacher to a fast food lunch of his choice, up to a $5.00 value. This activity is highly motivating for junior high school students with emotional disorders. They complete as many assignments as they can so they have as many chances as possible to win.

AUTHOR/SCIENTIST CHAIR

Audience: Upper elementary.

Objective: To encourage positive oral communication, build self-esteem, and promote positive attention.

Materials: A chair.

Description: Devote 10 minutes at the beginning or end of the writer's workshop or science period to this activity. During *Author's Chair*, a student volunteer shares an original piece of writing with the class, asking for feedback and ways to improve specifics (for example, dialogue, and description). During *Scientist's Chair*, a student volunteer shares an article, drawing, cartoon, poem, essay, experiment, research, song, interview book, video vignette, or some other topic of their choice relating to science.

Use: Specific classroom implementation to be completed by the selecting teacher.

When: Allocate 10 minutes at the end of either the writer's workshop or science period.

Where: In the classroom.

How: At the beginning of the year the teacher models the use of the *Author's Chair* by sharing with the class an original piece of their writing and asks the students to look for a particular idea or concept in the work to discuss and share. The science teacher models the *Scientist's Chair* activity, for example by sharing the history of the rain stick as an attention-getting device, during the unit on acoustics.

BEEBE'S BUCKS

Audience: Junior high school.

Objective: To encourage positive behavior in the classroom.

Materials: Precopy and precut green coupons that are valued at $1.00 apiece. Small prizes such as books, pencils, pens, and gift certificates are awarded.

Description: Students earn *Beebe Bucks* for any good behavior, for example, sharing, staying on task, exemplifying cooperation, kindness, and helpfulness.

Use: Specific classroom implementation to be completed by the selecting teacher

When: Use this activity during structured and unstructured time.

Where: Use it at break time, and lunch time, or in the classroom, library, or garden.

How: Pass out these *bucks* (coupons) at any time to students who are engaging in appropriate behavior. This positive reinforcement of commendable behavior encourages others to participate in proper behavior. At the end of the month, or when students have accumulated enough money, the teacher leads an auction where the students bid for desired prizes.

BOOST FOR HOMEWORK

Audience: Elementary.

Objective: To learn time-management skills.

Materials: A weekly calendar.

Description: Students are given a weekly calendar to write down things they need to do. All homework assignments should be written on this calendar.   When the homework is turned in, the assignment can be checked off.

Use: Specific classroom implementation to be completed by the selecting teacher.

When: This is used every day during class, once a procedure and routine are established.

Where: The classroom.

How: At school the students have a lot of things they need to remember. They should be taught how to organize themselves with a calendar. It is self-rewarding when you remember to look at your calendar and mark off the homework you have completed. As the end of the day rolls around, the teacher marks all the required homework on a calendar that looks just like the one that the students have. It is designed for the overhead so the students can see how the assignments should be written down. The teacher needs to point to the day and the week. After this has been done for awhile, the class remembers to write down their homework assignments in their calendars.

BRAIN FOOD

Audience: Elementary.

Objective: To encourage students to participate in the classroom.

Materials: Organic sugarless gummy bears or other nutritious small treats.

Description: When a child volunteers to read aloud, attempts to do a problem, or answers a question, the child gets a piece of *brain food. Brain Food* can also be used as encouragement when students have a hard task they must complete (like a state test).

Use: Specific classroom implementation to be completed by the selecting teacher.

When: Throughout the school day, any time during instruction.

Where: Any instructional area of the school.

How: At the beginning of the school year, the teacher tells the students that they need their brains to do the work required of them while in school. Sometimes their brains need a little *energy* to help keep them thinking. Whenever a child volunteers to read aloud, do a problem for the class, or give an answer to a question, give the child a piece of *brain food.* Even if he or she requires some help in giving an answer, the child still gets a piece of *brain food.* What's important is that, with or without the support of another classmate or the teacher, the child attempts to do the problem. *Brain food* can also be used as encouragement when students have to do a hard task or some task that requires a lot of concentration.

Caution: Be careful not to overdo it with the treats. Hand out the *brain food* sparingly and the occasion will become more special and meaningful to the children.

BRAVO POINT SYSTEM

Audience: Elementary.

Objective: To encourage positive behavior in the classroom.

Materials: Half sheet of paper lining out a schedule with time blocks, a pencil.

Description: When a child follows classroom rules and meets his or her individual behavior goals.

Use: Specific classroom implementation to be completed by the selecting teacher.

When: To be used throughout the day.

Where: This activity can be used anywhere on the school campus.

How: The school day is broken down into two time blocks—morning, before lunch and afternoon, after lunch. During each time block, a student can earn 0, 5, or 10 points for following classroom rules or meeting an individual goal. Points are assigned as follows:

10 points—student met the goal and followed classroom rules 100 percent of the time block

5 points—student met the goal and followed classroom rules 50 percent of the time block

0 points—student met the goal and followed classroom rules less than 50 percent of the time block

At the end of each time block, each student will award himself or herself the 0 to 10 points earned for following rules and attending to his or her individual goal during that time block. Individual goals should be written for one month periods or four weeks. Individual goals can highlight appropriate behavior reinforcements, such as turning in homework, having materials ready before class begins, and keeping a clean and orderly desk, to inappropriate behaviors such as not interrupting in class. The student records his or her points in the appropriate space on the daily point sheet (see sample). The maximum number of points attainable is 20 per day. The teacher checks the student's points and, if in agreement with the self-evaluation, the teacher praises the student for his or her honest and accurate self-evaluation and points are recorded on the point sheet. If the teacher does not agree with the student's self-evaluation, the teacher discusses the evaluation with the student, and the student adjusts his or her rating, either higher or lower to match the teacher's rating. Points are totaled at the end of the week and depending on the point totals, students choose a reward determined by the class. Reward time is usually on Friday afternoon. Rewards such as free computer time or a free homework pass are the most successful.

Bravo System Daily Point Sheet

Monday Date:	Tuesday Date:	Wednesday Date:	Thursday Date:	Friday Date:
Goal—Not talking to friends during class time Follows class rules	Goal—Not talking to friends during class time Follows class rules	Goal—Not talking to friends during class time Follows class rules	Goal—Not talking to friends during class time Follows class rules	Goal—Not talking to friends during class time Follows class rules
Morning points 10, 5, 0				
Afternoon points 10, 5, 0				
Total	Total	Total	Total	Total
				GRAND TOTAL

Note: It appears that checking the students point sheets can be time consuming. However, it takes less than a minute if the point sheet is displayed on the student's desk. You know if a discrepancy exists in the scoring because of "good-old-kid-watching." Keep students honest by doing a spot-check and docking points occasionally to send a message to the other students to stay on track.

CAMPUS STEWARDS

Audience: Elementary and junior high school.

Objective: To encourage students to keep the campus clean.

Materials: Large garbage bags and garbage containers. Awards and/or rewards for class participation.

Description: The purpose of Campus Stewards is to encourage ecological stewardship, foster inclusion and social skills, and promote responsibility for the school community and environment. Campus Stewards is a whole-school project with all classes participating. Goals and guidelines are established by a representative student committee, with staff supervision.

Use: Specific classroom implementation to be completed by the selecting teacher.

When: Throughout the school year each class is assigned a specific period of time when the class is responsible for picking up litter, keeping the campus clean, perhaps planting some native plants, and/or tending a garden near their classroom.

Where: The campus area for this activity is determined by the student committee.

How: The project is managed by the campus steward's committee, composed of class representatives and one or more supervising teachers. Each class assumes responsibility for determining how it can accomplish the overall goals and responsibilities. Thus, each class has the opportunity to practice organizational and leadership skills. Individual classes make their own decisions about how they reward themselves for their stewardship and teamwork. The reward might be a field trip to an ecological reserve, a nature museum, or some other site relevant to environmental awareness. The campus steward's committee can sponsor a whole-school cleanup and campus award celebration at the end of the year to honor everyone's participation.

CAUGHT BEING GOOD

Audience: Elementary.

Objective: To encourage positive behavior.

Materials: Decorated bulletin board (blue background with *star* trimmed borders with the title letters—*CAUGHT BEING GOOD*, and yellow 5 × 7 index cards (for inscribing student's name, date, comments and explanations, or a star).

Description: Recognition and praise provided by the teacher for various children who are caught being good.

Use: Specific classroom implementation to be completed by the selecting teacher.

When: Anytime during class time.

Where: On the bulletin board in the classroom.

How: At the beginning of the school year, the teacher decorates a *Caught Being Good* bulletin board in the classroom. The teacher explains to the children about the ongoing reward system during the school year. The teacher clearly explains about the ground rules for recognizing and praising positive behavior on a daily basis. They are

   (1) follow classroom rules,

   (2) work hard and do well in academic areas,

   (3) display positive behavior and attitude,

   (4) show respect toward peers and staff, and

   (5) be kind and helpful.

At the end of class, the teacher announces who was *caught being good* and posts the filled-in index card(s) on the bulletin board. The number of cards will be increased as the days go by. At the end of the week, the teacher removes them from the board and puts them in the students' folders to take home. The students' parents can recognize their child's good behavior in class and continue to provide the child additional praise at home.

CEO'S

Audience: Upper elementary and junior high school.

Objective: To learn time management skills.

Materials: Spiral-bound weekly/monthly planner.

Descriptions: Students use the planner to organize their school schedule and keep track of important dates, homework assignments, and grades.

Use: Specific classroom implementation to be completed by the selecting teacher.

When: Throughout the school day.

Where: This is used in each classroom.

How: At the beginning of each term, students are instructed by the homeroom teacher on the use of a weekly/monthly planner during the study skills unit. Students learn organization skills by maintaining a record of daily homework assignments in the week-at-a-glance section of the planner; long term goals such as exam dates, grades, and project due dates are maintained in the month-at-a-glance section of the planner. A daily *to do* list is a helpful reminder of the day's short-term goals. Once a week, the homeroom teacher instructs students to reflect on the organizational skills practiced during the past week by filling out a self-evaluation of school behaviors sheet presented in class (see My Progress Goals from Appendix 5). Each week the student can self-monitor the strategies of model student behavior and organization, and assess their strengths and note areas that need improvement. Goal setting and taking charge of responsibilities empower the students to be their own Chief Executive Officer or CEO.

CHANCE TICKETS

Audience: Elementary.

Objective: To maintain classroom rules and procedures.

Materials: Copies of Monopoly *Chance Tickets* (color coded) and special prizes.

Description: When a student is following the procedures and rules, the teacher hands out a *Chance Ticket* to that student. The students are able to use these chance tickets to receive prizes.

Use : Specific classroom implementation to be completed by the selecting teacher.

When: The teacher passes these tickets out to all students, throughout the day. They are passed out, before school starts, during class, recess, lunch, and after school.

Where: Anywhere on school grounds.

How: At the beginning of the school year, the teacher establishes the procedures and the rules. Then the teacher explains the *Chance Tickets* and other rewards. The teacher uses the chance tickets throughout the year to help consistently reinforce the procedures and rules. The students have two choices for how to use their chance tickets. The first choice is to put any amount of tickets into the daily drawing (name on the back of ticket) for prizes. If the class as a whole earns five stars that day for good classroom behavior, the teacher picks two chance tickets. If the class earns more than five stars then each increment of five increases the amount of tickets picked. The second choice is for the students to save their tickets for the class store on Fridays. Each ticket is worth 25 cents. The chance tickets are color coded each week, so the students start fresh every Monday.

CHARACTERS

Audience: Elementary.

Objective: To encourage participation in classroom.

Materials: Books, costumes, and a poster.

Description: Every other month, students present their book report in front of the class as their favorite character in the story. Students dress and act like the character as they explain the story. The classmates are allowed to share three comments with the character or ask three questions.

Use: Specific classroom implementation to be completed by the selecting teacher.

When: It is on a rotating schedule, depending on the amount of students in a class. For example, if a teacher has 28 students, he or she has seven students present their characters every Friday. Students can perform on the same week each month.

Where: This is to be done in their classroom.

How: At the beginning of the school year, the teacher makes a poster and puts it on the wall. The poster has each student's name on it and every time he or she presents a book report the child gets to write down the name of his or her book, character and the date it was performed. The procedures and rules are set in place prior to any presentations.

Variation: Instead of a scheduled presentation each Friday, students can sign up for *character Friday* and earn extra credit.

CHOOSE A CARD

Audience: Elementary.

Objective: To reinforce positive classroom behavior.

Materials: Trading cards of all types, (cartoons, sports, television, and celebrities) and charts for students to fill out.

Description: Students fill out a chart with the teacher. The chart is a simple contract that has a list of three behavioral, social, or academic goals determined by the student and approved by the teacher. This activity is used as a reinforcement for classroom social and academic behavior.

Use: Specific classroom implementation to be completed by the selecting teacher.

When: To be used weekly in the classroom.

Where: In the classroom setting only, unless the goal involves outside activities.

How: GOAL: During class when the teacher is talking, I will not touch or poke my classmates. Goals are checked off at the end of each day—circle *Yes* = 1 point and *No* = 0 points. Add up the points daily. Students can earn a grand total of 15 points per week or 3 points a day if they meet all their objectives. At the end of the week, students figure out the number of completed goals and objectives. If the student completes 10 to 15 points he or she can choose three trading cards; if a student earns 7 to 10 points the child can choose two trading cards; 5 to 7 points he or she can choose one trading card; less than 5 points and the child is not eligible to choose a trading card. The students trade or play with the cards during recess and free time. If need be, the teacher and student can reevaluate the chart and pick more realistic goals. Stickers or other objects can serve as substitutions for the cards. Using sports cards alone does not work because you leave out the incentive for some students. When you have a wide selection of cards all students want to participate. Goals and objectives should be reviewed after a month's time. The teacher can photocopy one sheet with four weekly charts—two on the front and two on the back (see below).

CHOOSE A CARD CHART

Day	Monday	Tuesday	Wednesday	Thursday	Friday
Goal #1	YES = 1 NO = 0	YES = 1 NO = 0	YES = 1 NO = 0	YES = 1 NO = 0	YES = 1 NO = 0
Goal # 2	YES = 1 NO = 0	YES = 1 NO = 0	YES = 1 NO = 0	YES = 1 NO = 0	YES = 1 NO = 0
Goal # 3	YES = 1 NO = 0	YES = 1 NO = 0	YES = 1 NO = 0	YES = 1 NO = 0	YES = 1 NO = 0
Total					
					Grand total

CLASSROOM STORE

Audience: All grades.

Objective: To encourage positive behavior in the classroom.

Materials: Play money and class store supplies.

Description: Students earn money, one dollar for every point, according to their individual behavior contracts. The students receive a check every two weeks for the daily points earned. Combine this activity with the biweekly Thursday math class so that the students use their math skills to figure out what amount they have earned. They can then cash their checks for merchandise in the classroom store.

Use: Specific classroom implementation to be completed by the selecting teacher.

When: Every other Friday.

Where: In the classroom.

How: Each of the students has individual behavioral goals identified with a point system. The students earn one dollar per point and can buy items or privileges from the classroom store. The items in the store are variably priced, with inexpensive and expensive items, so that everyone can purchase something. There are also some larger items priced to require several weeks of positive behavior points. The items can be purchased new, from garage sales, or donated from students, friends, family, or local businesses. It is important to evaluate student likes and dislikes early in the year so the store can be stocked accordingly. A manager role (store manager) can be assigned to a student who is then responsible for managing the store.

COLORED CARDS

Audience: Elementary.

Objective: To reinforce positive classroom behavior.

Materials: Five (5) different colored cards and a pocket chart.

Description: Each child has his or her name on a pocket chart. There are five different cards behind each name. The cards range from a smiling face to a sad face. Everyone starts out with the smiley face card. When an infraction occurs, the child committing the infraction is asked to go to the chart and change his or her card to the next card. Students earn positive cards through good behavior. The teacher is the only one who can change a card and students cannot ask about whether a card can be changed.

Use: Specific classroom implementation to be completed by the selecting teacher.

When: Throughout the school day.

Where: In the classroom setting. Behavior on the playground or at lunch does not affect card changes.

How: Set up expectations and explain the card system in the beginning of your first week of school. The consequences of the cards are as follows:

HAPPY FACE:	Recognition at end of class for positive behavior.
SLIGHT SMILE:	Good overall behavior—a minor slip up.
NO EXPRESSION:	Time taken away from free time.
FROWNING FACE:	Time taken away and a note home to parents.
SAD FACE:	Time taken away, a note and a call home to parents, and a parent conference if behavior continues for more than a few days. *You can add cards if you want to extend the consequences or you can make the consequences more specific.*

Note: This behavioral approach needs a calm and very balanced teacher to prevent students who have behavioral issues from always receiving a Frowning or Sad Face. Students can perceive this system to be unfair and subjective, so be mindful to encourage appropriate behavior and acknowledge students throughout the day.

EARN THE ACTIVITY OF YOUR CHOICE

Audience: Lower elementary.

Objective: To reinforce positive behavior.

Materials: Record sheets with each student's name. Individual and creative certificates rewarded.

Description: Students earn points based on behavior, attitude, effort, and cooperation on a daily basis. At the end of the week, scores are evaluated and if a student has scored high enough points, then he or she can select an activity of their choice.

Use: Specific classroom implementation to be completed by the selecting teacher.

When: This should be used during normal class time.

Where: It can be used in the classroom, the library, physical education class, inclusion class, and anywhere instruction is being given.

How: There are 25 points possible for each day. Four points are awarded for each activity time in the morning and five points for the afternoon time. The daily points are recorded on a chart and sent home for parents to see each day. At the end of the week, if the child has scored in the 18–25 category all week, he or she can enjoy an activity choice on Friday afternoons. The following values explain the point system:

22–25: Excellent—works hard with almost perfect behavior and terrific effort.

18–21: Good—works steady with some off-task and/or fairly consistent behavior.

14–17: OK—works inconsistently with little effort and/or has some behavior problems

10–13: Poor—works very little and/or has very poor behavior.

0–9: Unsatisfactory—call to parents and a note sent home, possible in class suspension or principal intercession.

FUN FRIDAY CHOICES

Audience: Elementary.

Objective: To reinforce positive behavior.

Materials: Behavior charts and a bag of prizes.

Description: During the duration of five days (Friday to Thursday) the teacher monitors the student's individual behavior and determines if he or she has a *smiley* day and records it in their individual chart. If the child has achieved four smiley days then at the end of the five-day period, he or she can draw out of the bag of prizes. The prizes consist of options such as no homework for a day, extra choice time, extra recess time, extra science or art time, or the appointment as *special helper*, which means that the student gets to run all the notes for a day to the office.

Use: Specific classroom implementation to be completed by the selecting teacher.

When: To be used during classroom time.

Where: This is to be used anywhere large group instruction takes place.

How: Every day the teacher monitors the students' behavior by using a behavior chart. Their behavior is recorded on the chart while throughout the day the teacher uses encouragement to promote good behavior. If the child has a good day, then at the end of the day the teacher gives him or her a *smiley* sticker to take home. On Friday morning, once five days have passed, the teacher announces the names of the students who had good weeks and allows them to draw out of the bag. They can share what they choose with the class and determine their special reward.

GIVING POSITIVES

Audience: Elementary through junior high school.

Objective: To reinforce positive behavior toward peers.

Materials: Koosh Ball, small stuffed animal, or other soft item that can be thrown.

Description: Positive statements given by all students to improve self-esteem and self-concept. This activity encourages belonging and connecting.

Use: Specific classroom implementation to be completed by the selecting teacher.

When: During class time, at the end of the day recommended.

Where: In the classroom.

How: The teacher begins by modeling how to give a specific positive statement. Teacher holds Koosh ball and says, "I want to give (student's name) a positive because . . . (insert specific statement) she showed diligence because she kept working on her essay even though she was becoming frustrated." The student acknowledges the positive and the teacher throws that student the Koosh Ball. The students continue the activity until all students have had a chance to give and receive a positive statement. Students may give two positives: one to a student who has already had a turn, followed by a positive to a student who has not had a turn.

Alternatives: Have the students state positive statements about themselves, or students make a positive statement about something they did successfully that day, or moving around the class students say something positive about the person to their left.

GOOD GROUP AWARD

Audience: Elementary.

Objective: To reinforce positive behavior using positive peer pressure.

Materials: Notebook, pencil, and scoreboard.

Description: The students are divided into groups of four. As a group, they earn points for exhibiting expected and positive behaviors. The groups change every five to six weeks.

Use: Specific classroom implementation to be completed by the selecting teacher.

When: Use during class time.

Where: Use in the classroom, library, or wherever instruction is being given.

How: At the beginning of the school semester, a point system is set up by the teacher, in which a given number of points will be issued for appropriate behavior. In addition to the point system, a reward system is also established. Points are given for all appropriate behavior. For example, a child receives 5 points for doing his or her homework or 10 points for doing his or her homework and having his or her parents sign it. All the points earned by a child are tallied and transferred to his or her assigned group. The first group to reach a predetermined number of points receives the preestablished reward, such as eating lunch in the classroom as opposed to the noisy cafeteria. After five or six weeks the groups change.

GROUP POINTS

Audience: Upper elementary.

Objective: To reinforce following directions and staying on task using positive peer pressure.

Materials: Small sticky notes on the desk of one member of each group plus a master sheet for teacher to record points.

Description: When one (or more) group(s) has followed the procedures for the activity in a timely and complete manner, the group gets a point. Record as you go by or quietly ask the recorder at that group to record a point for the group. At the same time, record a point on the master sheet. This double recording reduces the possibility of a complaint about inaccuracy or unfairness.

Use: Specific classroom implementation to be completed by the selecting teacher.

When: During work time, special activities, or transitions.

Where: In the classroom, or special activities, out of the classroom.

How: At the beginning of the year, the teacher describes the behavior that is expected. He/she explains that each group receives points when they are demonstrating the expected behavior. Role-playing by the teacher and a few brave volunteers helps demonstrate the expected group behavior. Then at the end of each week, the group with the most points has the privilege of choosing a class game, or requesting a preferred activity such as art or music. If you prefer to target the group more exclusively, you can give each group member a turn at the *grab bag* (with pencils and goodies in it), give them a short, free-choice period, or provide a special snack.

This system provides opportunities for special-needs students to participate in earning a group or a class reward. It is important to change the groupings every month or six weeks to keep all students involved and to avoid developing a group that is *good* at getting all the points.

HOMEWORK PASS

Audience: Elementary through junior high school.

Objective: To reinforce time-management skills (turning homework in on time).

Materials: Small slips of paper printed with *Homework Pass*.

Description: Passes issued and signed by the teacher that allow a student to skip one non-vital homework assignment and still be given the points for that assignment.

Use: Specific classroom implementation to be completed by the selecting teacher.

When: These can be turned in during the daily homework pick-up, in lieu of the assigned work.

Where: These will be used in the classroom.

How: Students can earn one (1) homework pass by turning in their daily homework on time for a predetermined amount of time (for example, three weeks in row). These assignments must be turned in complete and on time. The teacher issues a *signed* homework pass when these conditions are met. The pass can then be used to turn in as a substitute for a homework assignment.

Caveats

- Homework pass cannot be used to replace any kind of project or long, writing assignment.
- The consecutively turned in homework assignments do need to be done completely.
- Students need to make an effort to do the work, but do not need to do it perfectly.
- Homework passes are non-transferable (cannot be given to a friend).
- Homework passes can be used once a week at the most, they cannot be saved up.
- It is at the teacher's discretion to accept passes; when assigning homework he or she can announce that the homework pass is not eligible for this assignment.

Note: Although homework is a vital part of the learning process, students will, at some time or another, miss assignments. With this activity, students who regularly turn in homework are rewarded, and others who do not may be motivated to try to do so.

INDIVIDUAL REWARDS

Audience: Elementary through junior high school (used at the high school level).

Objective: To motivate learning skills.

Materials: Predeveloped chart or graph for students to record their scores.

Description: A student can record her or his score onto the chart to see her or his progress on class quizzes. The challenge is for the student to improve his or her score.

Use: Specific classroom implementation to be completed by the selecting teacher.

When: Use during weekly quizzes or any other subject where you or the student want to measure their improvement.

Where: Use in the classroom.

How: Within the first month of the school year, identify the students who you see need more motivation in a subject area. In that subject the teacher then gives weekly assignments to help the student assess their learning. By doing this, the student keeps track of his progress by recording the results on the chart. Since the student is keeping track of his own progress, he internalizes his own success and is motivated to continue the learning process. Of course, the teacher needs to praise the student for his or her good work and for doing extra to improve their skills, motivation, and perseverance to task.

KILL THE CURIOSITY

Audience: Upper elementary through junior high school (used at the high school level).

Objective: To reinforce and teach discussion techniques and management.

Materials: None

Description: The teacher provides open discussion for the students about educational issues to stimulate and satisfy the students' curiosity.

Use: Specific classroom implementation to be completed by the selecting teacher.

When: This is to be used during class time.

Where: This is to be used in the classroom.

How: At the beginning of the school year, the teacher makes a poster and puts it on the wall. The information contained on the poster is the ground rules for open discussions about any educational issue. The teacher also explains the ground rules clearly to the class. During class time, the students can bring up any issue that he or she is curious about. It can be from today's newspaper or another source. It can also be an interesting conversational issue derived from one of the teacher's lectures. A student might spark an idea from a question or comment; the teacher then asks that student to tell the rest of the class about the issue, and the teacher gives the class the opportunity to hold a discussion. The teacher is also involved in the discussion. There are five ground rules for the open discussion. The ground rules are

(1) each open discussion is limited to 5 minutes,

(2) one person speaks at a time,

(3) open discussion cannot be held during the last 10 minutes of class time,

(4) a limit of two issues per period, and

(5) personal issues are not appropriate for discussion.

KIND AND CARING TICKETS

Audience: Elementary.

Objective: To promote positive peer relationships.

Materials: Tickets and special activity or prizes.

Description: When a child acts kind and caring toward another child or to the teacher, the child is given a *Kind and Caring Ticket*. At the end of the week, all students who have kind and caring tickets put their names on the tickets that are put into a jar for a raffle.

Use: Specific classroom implementation to be completed by the selecting teacher.

When: Before school, throughout the school day, at recess, lunch, and after school.

Where: Anywhere at school including the classroom, playground, and library.

How: At the beginning of the school year, the teacher establishes with the class what is considered kind and caring behavior. Kind and caring acts range from lending someone a pencil, to helping someone with a task, to working quietly and being on task. Whenever a child is *caught* being kind and caring, the child is given a *kind and caring ticket. Kind and caring tickets* can be given by either a child or the teacher. At the end of the week, all *kind and caring tickets* are put into a jar for a raffle. The rewards can range from a special privilege to a prize.

LARGE GROUP RHYTHM

Audience: Lower elementary.

Objective: To teach students to focus in a group.

Materials: A strong voice.

Description: The students are in large groups and are expected to be ready to begin the lesson.

Use: Specific classroom implementation to be completed by the selecting teacher.

When: Use during circle time.

Where: Use in the classroom.

How: Use this after the students sit down on the carpet, or use this anytime in order to refocus them or to remind them of expected behavior. The teacher chants in a clear voice, "Put your hands in your lap by the time I . . . *snap, snap, snap.*" The teacher snaps his or her fingers each time that the word *snap* is said.

LARGE GROUP SINGING

Audience: Lower elementary.

Objective: To teach students to focus in a large group.

Materials: A strong voice.

Description: The students are grouped together as a whole class.

Use: Specific classroom implementation to be completed by the selecting teacher.

When: Use when the teacher wants to call the class back together after an activity. Use to focus students in the morning and after transitions.

Where: Use during circle time.

How: At the beginning of circle time, or anytime if it is necessary to call students to the carpet, the teacher sings to the tune of *If you're happy and you know it*. The teacher replaces the words in the song with the command words . . . "put your bottoms on the rug, on the rug. Put your bottoms on the rug, put your bottoms on the rug, put your bottoms on the rug, on the rug."

LENDER BINDER

Audience:	Upper elementary through high school.
Objective:	To encourage students to bring supplies to class.
Materials:	A raggedy, old binder that the teacher likes because of its completeness, but is unattractive to the students because of the way it looks. It is old, ugly, smells a bit, the pencils in the pencil case are chewed up, and the paper in the back is wrinkled, or consists of the back sides of duplicated documents.
Description:	Students who do not bring their binder to school must use and carry *the lender binder*. This logical consequence allows them to complete their work but encourages them to bring their own. I heard about this idea from Dr. Anita Archer.
Use:	Specific classroom implementation to be completed by the selecting teacher.
When:	When students leave their binder at home.
Where:	The binder is kept in class.
How:	At the beginning of the year the teacher creates several *lender binders* using the least desirable, but still functional supplies. When students forget their binders, they use a lender binder for that day. At the end of the day they take the pages they wrote on in the lender binder out and bring them home to copy into their regular binder.
Troubleshooting:	Don't make the binder so undesirable that it is humiliating; otherwise, you can create behavior problems in reaction. For example, it might be funny to put a picture of Barney on the lender binder's cover, but a child might feel humiliated having to carry it around. Think about the purpose of the activity—to encourage the student to be more responsible for his or her behavior.

LONG JOURNEY HOME

Audience: Elementary.

Objective: To reinforce classroom rules and time-management skills using positive peer pressure.

Materials: A large map of an era of time (the West during the migration, or Christopher Columbus's voyage), stamps or stickers, and something that could represent a vehicle that was used for travel during that time period.

Description: The students are placed in groups that represent teams, a family or a crew who journey across the time era to reach their final destination. The only way that the team can travel or gain miles is by working together to make certain that each person in their group is following classroom rules and turning in her or his daily and weekly homework assignments.

Use: Specific classroom implementation to be completed by the selecting teacher.

When: Use during classroom time.

Where: Use in the classroom.

How: At the beginning of the year, the teacher places the kids into small groups of four or five deciding what era they will be traveling through, and whether their group represents a family, a crew, or teammates. There is a huge map of the area and of the era on one wall in the classroom with each group's designated vehicle at the starting position. Each group is assigned different colors to represent their group and their vehicle. For example, if you decide to travel through the Midwest during the migration then their vehicle is a wagon with horses. The only way for the group to gain miles is to follow classroom rules and make sure each member turns in her or his homework. If all the rules are followed and homework is turned in, the group's vehicle travels a certain amount of miles. The point is for the group to work together and to support each member, and by the end of the month, semester, and/or year each group eventually completes their journey. Adjust the amount of time to correspond with the developmental age of the students. One type of reward for this activity is a pizza party with the teacher, the school principal or another very special person to the students.

Note: Assign a homework buddy so that the team does not lose travel time because of absences.

LOOK AT ME

Audience: Upper elementary through high school.

Objective: To teach students how to ask for positive attention.

Materials: Look at Me cards—two cards laminated with the statement *notice me please* written in ASL (American Sign Language).

Description: Students have the opportunity to tell the class about something that they did that made them feel proud or good. This helps students express positive praise to themselves and helps to develop self-esteem.

Use: Specific classroom implementation to be completed by the selecting teacher.

When: Use at the beginning of class.

Where: Use in the classroom.

How: At the beginning of the school year, the teacher makes a poster and puts two cards in its pocket on the wall. The information printed on the poster shows the ground rules for using the Look at Me cards. The teacher explains the ground rules clearly to the class. During the beginning of the class when students wish to share their success or news about themselves, they can pick a card from the wall and put it on their desk. The teacher then grants the student permission to share with the class any good things or acts that they want to discuss. The *good thing* can involve sports, news, good grades, or helping others. The ground rules for this activity include:

(1) only two students sharing per day;

(2) sharing only good or positive things about themselves;

(3) whole class waves their hands after each positive comment; and

(4) each sharing is limited to 1 to 2 minutes.

LUNCH WITH TEACHER

Audience: Elementary.

Objective: To reinforce positive behavior and to follow class rules using positive peer pressure.

Materials: None.

Description: When the whole class follows the class rules each period, the teacher pastes a star sticker on a poster named *Lunch Together*. When the class accumulates 50 stars, the teacher has lunch with the class. The class can choose whether to have lunch with their teacher at the cafeteria or in the classroom.

Use: Specific classroom implementation to be completed by the selecting teacher.

When: During the lunch time.

Where: At the cafeteria or in the classroom.

How: At the beginning of the year, the teacher establishes the class rules or expectations. The rules can range from raising your hand before speaking, to keeping your hands to yourself, to using appropriate language, to staying in your seat. The teacher makes a poster and teaches the class how to earn a star sticker. Each star sticker has a sequential number on it. Whenever the number reaches 50, the class can discuss the day and the place they want to have the lunch with the teacher.

Note: I would suggest the teacher brings some extra *goodies* to the luncheon as an additional reward for following class rules. Also, the teacher should make certain they can afford this, or have parents chip in, so there is ample food to go around.

MARBLES IN A JAR

Audience: Elementary.

Objective: To reinforce positive behavior using positive peer pressure.

Description: This is a group contingency behavior management program in which the teacher rates class behavior each period or during each activity. The teacher looks for on-task behaviors and group cooperation.

Materials: A bag of marbles and a jar.

Use: Specific classroom implementation to be completed by the selecting teacher.

When: During class time.

Where: In the classroom.

How: For each individual instructional period such as reading, language arts, and math, the class can receive zero to five points during the course of the day. The teacher uses a bag of marbles and a jar to keep track of points earned by the class, putting a marble into a jar each time the class earns a point. Each marble is worth one minute of free time to use at the end of the month to watch a video, or for another free time activity. This activity can be used all year.

Note: This group contingency reward system helps improve student behavior. Still, it is a good idea to combine group and individual contingencies when necessary.

MR. STEVEN'S BUCKS

Audience: Elementary.

Objective: To encourage students to offer help and to keep the class and school clean.

Materials: Premade dollar bills made of construction paper.

Description: Students earn the bucks by performing supplementary school tasks such as being a trustee (tutor), work grader, lunchtime helper, and so on. In order to be eligible for the above jobs, a student must be current with his or her work and not have any behavior infractions for the week. Students then are able to buy special privileges with these bucks such as obtain a bathroom pass, earn the ability to eat and drink during class (specified food and times), select free-choice time, and even buy their way out of garbage collection during recess (given to students who do not turn in math homework, or commit behavior infractions).

Use: Specific classroom implementation to be completed by the selecting teacher.

When: During the school day.

Where: In the classroom or wherever instruction takes place.

How: There is a chart on the board that states the amount the students earn for tasks performed and the cost of the privileges. Mr. Stevens sets up a time on Fridays to pay students for work performed during the week. The amount earned is written on the bill, such as eight dollars. Throughout the week, the work performed is usually marked on either the students' individual work assignment sheets, or student's names are put on the board. Students usually pay for the privilege at the time the request is made. The teacher simply crosses out the old amount on the bill and writes in the new amount, cutting down on interruptions to the class and conserving paper. For instance, if the privilege to eat or drink during class is worth six of Mr. Steven's Bucks, then the teacher crosses out the amount on the current bill, say eight bucks, and now the student has two bucks left. During the next week based on their eligibility, the student can add more bucks and save them up or use them for another privilege.

NAME IN THE HEART BOX

Audience: Elementary.

Objective: To encourage students to model positive classroom behavior.

Materials: Markers, crayons, colored pencils, stickers, a shoe or comparable size box.

Description: When you notice a student in your class displaying positive behavior or following directions when it is hard for the other children to do so, the student is allowed to put his or her name in the *Heart Box*. To make a heart box use a shoe box or a comparable size box and then wrap it with construction paper. Have students decorate it with heart stickers or draw hearts.

Use: Specific classroom implementation to be completed by the selecting teacher.

When: During class time.

Where: This is to be used in the classroom when a student's behavior is exceptionally good.

How: At the time the behavior is noticed, the teacher thanks the student for the behavior (be specific) and announces very loudly so that the whole class can hear that the student may put his or her name in the heart box. The student also gets to choose a sticker or *goody* at the end of the day to take home with her or him.

NUMBER CLUB

Audience: Elementary.

Objective: To keep students busy practicing skills while they are waiting for teacher assistance.

Materials: Folders, graph paper, banners or flags, and bright markers.

Description: Use when a child is unable to do an assignment and is waiting for assistance from the teacher. The child takes out his or her *Number Club Folder* and practices an exercise that the teacher has explained in great detail.

Use: Specific classroom implementation to be completed by the selecting teacher.

When: Use during directed learning activities.

Where: Use in the classroom.

How: At the beginning of a math unit the teacher introduces the new folder. The teacher establishes guidelines of appropriate times for students to pull out their number club folder. For example, if we are beginning a unit on the number chart, students will receive a folder with a bunch of graph pages. The student writes all the numbers from 1 to 1,000. As the student completes each level, for example level 200, their name is placed on a flag on the wall that says "200 Number Club." This allows a student to keep on task as well and does not take away from the student's learning time. This can also be adapted for other subjects, for example, *Rhyming Word Club* for language arts.

OLYMPICS

Audience: Junior high school (used at the high school level).

Objective: To encourage students to change clothes quickly after P.E.

Materials: Gold, silver, and bronze paper medals.

Description: When students change clothes quickly after Physical Education class is over, they go to a designated place where a line forms in preparation for walking to the next classroom. The different colored medals are passed out to each student when she or he arrives and stands in line. A student who arrives and stands in line within 3 minutes after P.E. class ends receives a gold medal, within 4 minutes receives a silver medal, within 5 minutes receives a bronze medal, and after 5 minutes the child does not receive a medal. Each month, the students receive prizes based on their earned gold medals.

Use: Specific classroom implementation to be completed by the selecting teacher.

When: Use during the time between the end of P.E. class and the next class.

Where: Use in the school area where the line is formed by the students arriving after they change their clothes.

How: At the beginning of the school year, the teacher sets up a poster describing the reward system and puts it on the wall in the classroom. The teacher also clearly explains this system to the class. Two silver medals are equal to one gold medal. Four bronze medals are equal to one gold medal. Two bronze medals are equal to one silver medal. At the end of each month, a child who has 18 gold medals earns the largest prize. A child who has 15 gold medals earns a large prize. A child with 12 gold medals earns a medium prize. A child with 11 gold medals or less does not earn a prize.

Note: Make certain that the prizes are cost effective. Do not reward with candy. Health bars or nutritional snacks are OK.

PASS CHALLENGE

Audience: Upper elementary through junior high school.

Objective: To encourage positive participation in classroom business.

Materials: None.

Description: A Pass Manager selected by the teacher is responsible for handing out passes during a semester. Specific ground rules are established by the teacher as to what actions qualify to receive a pass. A challenge can take place whenever a student feels that the Pass Manager is distributing the passes in an unfair manner.

Use: Specific classroom implementation to be completed by the selecting teacher.

When: As needed.

Where: In the classroom.

How: When the Pass Manager is accused of being unfair by one of the students, a mock courtroom setting is used to handle the challenge (see Class Meetings in Part I, Chapter 6, for added thoughts on this activity). The manager handles the prosecution and the challenger handles the defense. Each side is allowed 2 minutes to present a case with the challenger going first. The class acts as the jury and has 2 minutes to decide on a verdict. The verdict is binding. In the case of a tie, the verdict goes to the prosecution.

PAY WELL TO THOSE WHO PLAY WELL

Audience: Elementary.

Objective: To encourage positive behavior at school.

Materials: Tickets or tokens. Small prizes such as pencils, erasers, and certificates of achievement used as rewards.

Description: When students are observed on campus behaving appropriately or doing something good, they are given a ticket or token. The student can then turn these tickets or tokens into the office in exchange for a prize.

Use: Specific classroom implementation to be completed by the selecting teacher.

When: Use weekly in the classroom.

Where: Use anywhere on the school campus.

How: At the beginning of the semester, the staff of the school set up a set of guidelines defining behaviors that they wish to see the children exhibit during their free time. They also set up a value system for each desired behavior. They then assign different colored tickets or tokens worth a given point value to each desired behavior. When a staff member sees a child performing a desired behavior during a free-time activity, he or she will be given a ticket appropriate to the behavior. When a child gets enough tickets, he or she can turn them into the office for a prize. The prizes are worth different point values so the child can buy the prize he or she wishes. Because a staff member can't watch all students all the time, this activity encourages students to behave well in the hopes that they may be *caught being good*.

PIZZA CHALLENGE

Audience: Upper elementary through junior high school.

Objective: To encourage the on-task behavior of an entire class.

Materials: Pictures of pizza slices laminated.

Description: The teacher sets up a "pizza board" where all the students can see you put up a slice of pizza. The class earns a slice of pizza when all students are on task. A completed pizza equals a class pizza party.

Use: Specific classroom implementation to be completed by the selecting teacher.

When: Throughout the school day.

Where: In the classroom.

How: You explain to the class that they can earn a slice of pizza on the chart for being on task and using time wisely. The teacher is the only one who determines when the slice goes on the chart, and the slice will not come down until the whole pizza is complete. Once the whole pizza is complete, the class is rewarded with a real pizza purchased by the teacher.

Note: Make certain that the pizza is at least 15 slices and earning a slice of pizza means that the class was *exceptionally good* that day. Exceptionally good can mean many different things from being actively engaged academically, to supporting one another in a kind and caring manner, to following directions the first time they were asked. Do not reward slices of pizza on a daily basis because the reward loses its impact. Be prepared to spend some "dough" on this reward if you chose to use it.

POPSICLE STICKS

Audience: Elementary through junior high school.

Objective: To encourage positive classroom behavior.

Materials: Popsicle sticks with students' names on them.

Description: At the beginning of each day, one student is chosen to be classroom manager. As classroom manager, the student monitors the behavior of the class during large group instruction. At the end of large group instruction, the classroom manager chooses two students who he or she felt were showing good behavior. These students are rewarded with such privileges as being the first to line up, the first to go out to lunch or recess, or the first to choose balls for recess.

Use: Specific classroom implementation to be completed by the selecting teacher.

When: Use during large group instruction.

Where: Use anywhere large group instruction takes place.

How: Every morning the classroom manager is chosen by the teacher at random from a drawing of all the popsicle sticks. The classroom manager monitors the behavior of the students during large group instruction. At the end of the instruction, the manager is asked to choose two students who exhibited appropriate behavior. The two students chosen will be given a privilege.

Caution: The teacher needs to monitor the behavior of the classroom manager. Setting up a few manager ground rules helps prevent favoritism (giving privileges to his or her best buddy).

PRIVILEGE AUCTION

Audience:	Elementary and middle school.
Objective:	To encourage students to help keep the classroom and school environment clean and organized.
Materials:	Play money and privilege coupons.
Description:	After students have completed their regular classroom chores, they have the opportunity to earn auction money by undertaking a set number of special assignments that go above and beyond normal student expectations. At the end of a specified period, the teacher holds an auction, and the students can use their money to bid on a variety of privileges. It is important to reemphasize that students are not eligible to earn auction money until after they have fulfilled their normal cleaning responsibilities. The purpose of the activity is to motivate students to keep their work areas clean, but it can be modified to encourage all sorts of behavior.
Use:	Specific classroom implementation to be completed by the selecting teacher.
When:	During class clean-up times, recesses, and break times.
Where:	In the classroom or on the playground.
How:	After telling the class the classroom cleanliness and organizational expectations, you explain that on such and such a date there will be a class auction, where special privileges will be auctioned off (explain an auction and then mark a date for it on the class calendar). The currency used in the auction is play money earned for work that goes beyond the normal student expectations. The teacher should display a poster that lists jobs that students can sign up for to earn money. These can be tasks like taking notes for the class binder, being a recorder for the class calendar, giving a new student a tour of the school, tutoring a classmate during lunch, looking after a student who is being picked on by other students at recess, and vacuuming the classroom during lunch.
Troubleshooting:	The teacher needs to find jobs for kids who want to work. You might need to go beyond the classroom to create those jobs. You could have students pick up trash, empty the recycling bins, assist the librarian, etc. The teacher also needs desirable privileges to auction off or there is not much incentive for the children to work. The privileges given also need to be designed to not increase misbehavior.

QUESTION BOX

Audience: Elementary through junior high school.

Objective: To encourage students to stay on-task during class time.

Materials: Small box or container.

Description: Students can use the question box to ask any question having to do with an academic subject area, current events, or school-related issues and interests. A designated time is set aside for a teacher-led discussion about finding the answers to the questions presented.

Use: Specific classroom implementation to be completed by the selecting teacher.

When: Use during class time.

Where: Use in the classroom.

How: At the beginning of the school year, the teacher or students design a box or container called the *Question Box*. Next to the box is a stack of small scratch paper and a pencil or pen. At any time during the school year, students can write down questions they have regarding an academic subject area or any other school-related issues. The students can choose to be recognized by writing their names or not. As a class, a time is set aside for the question box. During this time about five questions (or more depending on time) are addressed at random and answered by the teacher or other students. Before getting started with this activity, the teacher shares the criteria for asking questions so students are clear on what types of questions are appropriate. If a student has a burning question in the box that is not addressed due to time constraints, assure that student that you will meet with her or him privately to discuss it.

Sample: While teaching a unit on the life cycle of the butterfly, the class quickly got off track with a myriad of questions. Though I was delighted with the student interest in the subject matter, I began to tangent off subject trying to answer all of their questions. The *question box* enables students to write their questions down and know that at the end of the day they will be addressed and answered. It also helps the teacher stay on task.

RED LIGHT–GREEN LIGHT

Audience: Elementary.

Objective: To teach students appropriate behaviors for different class activities.

Materials: A lamp with three separate light sources, red, yellow, and green bulbs (like a stop light).

Description: Explanation in the *How* section below.

Use: Specific classroom implementation to be completed by the selecting teacher.

When: Use during class time.

Where: Use in the classroom.

How: At the beginning of the school year, the class comes up with a list of appropriate behaviors for each stoplight color. The teacher also establishes rewards and consequences for abiding by the colored lights. For example, the red light means that students cannot talk and must raise their hands to leave their seats. The yellow light means that students can talk with their "one inch" voice (a volume for just the person next to them to hear) and can get out of their seats to get what they need. The green light means that students can use their table voices and work quietly anywhere in the room.

RESOURCE POINTS

Audience: Upper elementary through junior high school.

Objective: To encourage positive classroom behavior.

Materials: Resource Point Sheet.

Description: Students collect points on a *Resource Point Sheet* that earns them tickets that can be used to purchase treats and school materials.

Use: Specific classroom implementation to be completed by the selecting teacher.

When: Daily.

Where: In each classroom, every period.

How: Each student keeps a weekly resource point sheet for each period of the day that the teacher fills out and initials. Students earn points for: *preparation* (2 points for having all materials, notebooks organized, and ready to work); *calendar* (2 points for writing all assignments down correctly and legibly on their calendars); *rules* (2 points for following all classroom rules); *on task* (3 points for working quietly and with good effort for the whole work period); *punctuality* (1 point for being seated, quiet, and ready to work by the last bell). If a student earns 7 to 10 points each day the student receives a ticket. With teacher approval, a ticket can also be earned for exceptional work in other classes. Five tickets is the maximum number that can be earned in a week and garners a big payoff, four tickets a lesser payoff, and so forth. Tickets are paid and spent only on the last day of the week. There are no IOU's, except when the teacher needs to purchase additional materials.

SELF-TALK

Audience: Elementary through junior high school.

Objective: To teach students self-confidence and to monitor their own behaviors.

Materials: None.

Description: The purpose of *Self-Talk* is to develop self-awareness and to become more attentive to the kinds of internal thoughts and messages that we all send to ourselves. Through discussion and the practice of positive *self-talk*, students learn to monitor their own internal messages, give themselves encouragement, and learn how to redirect their behavior.

Use: Specific classroom implementation to be completed by the selecting teacher.

When: *Self-Talk* may be introduced in a class at any time that seems appropriate to the teacher. It might be included in a social studies, health education lesson, or in a discussion about classroom management.

Where: Initial discussion is in the classroom, but we take *self-talk* with us everywhere we go.

How: Ask students to think about the kinds of things they say to themselves under various circumstances. For example, "What do you say to yourself, in your head or under your breath, when you make a mistake?" "What do you say to yourself, in your head or under your breath, when you do something that you like, when you complete an assignment, or score a point in a game?" Working in pairs, share with your partner some of the things that you say to yourself when you do something great and when you do something you don't like.

Call on a member of each pair and ask the student to share some of their self-talk examples with the class.

Discuss the benefits of positive self-talk and the downside of negative self-talk.

How do our thoughts affect how we feel and what we do?

How can self-talk help us redirect our behavior?

What is the benefit of self-direction in the classroom, on the playground, or elsewhere?

Generate examples of self-talk: "Good Job, Marissa!" "Wow, I got it now!"

SHARING THE NEWS

Audience: Lower elementary.

Objective: To allow for positive peer attention.

Materials: Up to the student who wants to bring something to share with the class or talk about himself or herself.

Description: Each student gets the opportunity to share his or her weekend news. This helps students to know when to talk about things other than school work so they can focus better during work times.

Use: Specific classroom implementation to be completed by the selecting teacher.

When: Every Monday, first thing in the morning.

Where: In class where students sit on their color carpet mat, circle and face each other.

How: The teacher allows the star leader of the week to start by sharing weekend news with classmates as well as the teacher. Then each student takes a turn clockwise to share news. The ground rules are as follows:

(1) each student can share his or her news for 2 minutes,

(2) no interruption during sharing time, and

(3) students are allowed to ask one question.

Note: Each week in our class we choose a star leader who is responsible for assuming various leadership roles assigned for that week. Examples range from peer assistance to mundane tasks like putting the chairs up on desks at the end of the school day.

SHARING TIME

Audience: Elementary.

Objective: To allow for positive peer attention.

Materials: Anything that the students wish to share with the class.

Description: Every Monday there is a sharing period when the students can share something that is important to them, whether it is an event or an item.

Use: Specific classroom implementation to be completed by the selecting teacher.

When: During class time.

Where: In the classroom.

How: The teacher discusses and hangs up a poster of the ground rules regarding the sharing time. The ground rules are as follows: No one interferes with the student while he/she is sharing, no one makes fun of anything that the sharing student feels is important to him/her, and each sharing person is allowed 3 to 5 minutes to share. During the sharing time, the students can bring into class any item that they feel is important to them, or they can just share an event that occurred and impacted them. There is the opportunity for several students to share during each week. After the sharing time, the teacher encourages the students to ask questions.

SHOW 'N' TELL

Audience: Lower elementary.

Objective: To allow for positive peer attention.

Materials: Various objects (toys, books, etc.).

Description: Showing and sharing provided by individual children about various things that relate to the educational issues discussed in class.

Use: Specific classroom implementation to be completed by the selecting teacher.

When: On a weekly basis during class time.

Where: In the classroom.

How: Based on the educational issues and/or monthly themes taught and discussed by the teacher in class during the week, the children have an opportunity to bring something from home for the Show 'n' Tell activity on their scheduled days. The teacher explains clearly about the ground rules for this activity. They are

(1) children are assigned a turn on specific days,

(2) one person speaks at a time,

(3) the activity is limited to 5 to 10 minutes,

(4) the audience has to raise their hands to ask questions, and

(5) there is a limit of two or three questions.

Assigned children explain, share, show, and answer questions about their subject. The teacher monitors and makes sure that everyone has a turn to ask questions. In addition, the teacher guides and assists whenever necessary throughout the show 'n' tell activity.

SMILEY FACES

Audience: Lower elementary.

Objective: To change negative behavior to positive classroom behavior.

Materials: Narrow slips of paper with a row of smiley faces, above each smiley face is a single word description of each period during the day (SSR, circle, math). You will also need a graph drawn with the days of the week along one side and the number of smiley faces along the other.

Description: This is an individualized, positive reward system worked out between the parents, the teacher and the student. When a student is on-task during the day, the teacher marks the smiley face corresponding to that time. For example, if a student is on-task during a guided reading group, the teacher makes an X over the face. At the end of the day, the teacher gives the student the slip and reviews where he or she earned a smiley face. The slip is taken home to be reviewed with the child's parents who also reinforce where the student earned the smiley faces. The teacher graphs the number of smiley faces the student receives for the day, and the graph is sent home at the end of the month.

Use: Specific classroom implementation to be completed by the selecting teacher.

When: Use continually during the school day.

Where: Use in every situation where the student participates.

How: This is set up with a student who is having a difficult time managing his or her behavior. It is used for a specific behavior (like working cooperatively) or this activity can focus on the students overall performance. It is set up at a conference with the student's parents, the student, and the teacher. Teacher and parent consistency are vital for this to work. The teacher needs to be mindful of completing the slips and the parent needs to remember to review it with the child at home. At the end of the month, the teacher reviews the graph with the student to show his or her progress and then sends it home for parental review.

SOAPBOX

Audience: Junior high school through high school level.

Objective: To encourage students to speak out on issues that are important to them.

Materials: Real or imaginary "soapbox" to stand on.

Description: Students are given 5 minutes to editorialize on a social topic of their choice to the captive audience of their peers and teachers.

Use: Specific classroom implementation to be completed by the selecting teacher.

When: Use during class time, preferably at the end of the period.

Where: This is probably more suitable for a social science, homeroom, or English class.

How: Newspapers and news shows are often ignored by today's teenagers. As an incentive to get students to observe and contemplate their society, students who see an issue in the paper or other news source, including the neighborhood grapevine, can have 5 minutes to get up on the proverbial *soapbox* and give their point of view of an issue or occurrence. Neither the class nor the teacher can interrupt during their time.

Students who bring an article into class or cite a source can put their name on a soapbox list. The teacher checks the list before the last 10 minutes of class.

Guidelines

- Inappropriate language cannot be used.
- Editorial cannot be focused on an individual peer or teacher.
- Everybody gives attention and respect to the speaker.
- Teacher should check out "sensitive" issues or topics that are frowned upon by the school and advise students before they are permitted to speak about them.

STAMP YOUR WAY TO GOOD BEHAVIOR

Audience: Elementary.

Objective: To encourage positive classroom behavior.

Materials: Small slips of paper and stamps.

Description: When a child is behaving appropriately, the teacher gives the child a slip of paper with a stamp on it. After collecting a specified amount of stamps, the student receives a special privilege.

Use: Specific classroom implementation to be completed by the selecting teacher.

When: Use during class time.

Where: Use in the classroom, library, or anywhere that instruction is being given.

How: At the beginning of the school year, the teacher sets up a privilege list indicating the number of stamped papers required to buy each privilege. The teacher also establishes a set of behaviors or rules that the students perform to earn a stamped paper. During the semester when the teacher observes the student behaving in the appropriate manner, the teacher issues the student a slip of paper with a stamp on it. The student can then spend those stamps to earn the predetermined privileges. Privileges include turning in one assignment late or going to the restroom without raising a hand. The privileges are established in relation to the rules of the classroom.

STAR JAR

Audience: Elementary.

Objective: To encourage on-task behavior.

Materials: Jar, slips of paper with star outline, and pencil or pen.

Description: Students are rewarded for on-task behavior on a random schedule.

Use: Specific classroom implementation to be completed by the selecting teacher.

When: Use this system when appropriate student behavior is desired from the whole group and incidence of the desired behavior is low.

Where: Use this system in the classroom.

How: The teacher has star slips and a pencil or pen in a basket that can easily be carried from one location to another. When the class is having difficulty settling down, the basket is brought out and a star is awarded to a student who is displaying the desired behavior. The student's name is written in the center of the star and the star is handed to the student. At the end of the lesson, the student deposits his star(s) in the jar. At recess time, slips of paper are drawn from the *Star Jar* and ball privileges (student gets to take class ball out to recess or at lunch time) are awarded on that basis. The more appropriate behavior the student displays, the better the chances are to receive ball privileges. Students are not allowed to ask for stars. This method proves to be very effective for achieving desirable behavior when several students in the class display undesirable behavior.

Variation: Privileges may vary accordingly to highlight a particular student or situation. The variation is left up to the teacher to assess.

STAR OF THE WEEK

Audience:	Elementary through junior high school.
Objective:	To allow for positive attention.
Materials:	One bulletin board decorated; this is used to place the student's picture and special things he or she wants displayed.
Description:	Each week a different student is chosen as *Star of the Week*. This is that student's week to shine.
Use:	Specific classroom implementation to be completed by the selecting teacher.
When:	Once a week a student is chosen. Display lasts a week.
Where:	In the classroom.
How:	Every student in the class is given the opportunity to bring in special pictures of himself or herself, their family, and places visited. The student is given time to talk about the pictures on Monday. Tuesday, the entire class will take the student's name and come up with a positive or strength for each letter in her or his name. Wednesday, the student gets to talk about her or his favorite things and activities. Thursday, the other students write a positive letter to the student telling the student what he or she likes about that student. Friday, the star student is able to bring in one special item and show it to the class. The entire theme is to build the self-esteem of the star student.

Note: This is especially good for elementary students. You may want to revise this for older students.

STARS, "DOLLARS," AND *LA TIENDITA*

Audience: Elementary.

Objective: To encourage positive behavior.

Materials: Dollar bills (play money), stickers and small toys for *la tiendita* (little store), and a board and chart for recording the awarded stars.

Description: Children receive stars for good behavior, for staying on task, for good work, and for other agreed upon actions. In my class, *la tiendita* is a popular math activity. Students can buy stickers, pencils and little toys with the play money they earn. The students receive one *dollar* for every five stars they earn.

Use: Specific classroom implementation to be completed by the selecting teacher.

When: Students can earn stars throughout the day. Their stars are totaled up at the end of the day and recorded on a chart.

Where: In the classroom or anywhere in the school (playground, library, cafeteria).

How: This can be ongoing or can be used for limited periods of time. Students receive stars for various activities and actions; for example, a student who remembers to say "please" or "thank you" spontaneously might get a star. Or a student who is nice to another student—by sharing or showing some kindness— might get a star. The stars for a specified period of time are totaled up and converted into dollars for *la tiendita*.

STICKERS FOR ALL SEASONS

Audience: Lower elementary.

Objective: To encourage positive behavior.

Materials: Paper chart, 8 × 11, and stickers (theme of the week).

Description: Teacher gives each student stickers at the end of class to recognize a variety of good behaviors or good work in the classroom.

Use: Specific classroom implementation to be completed by the selecting teacher.

When: Use during the end of class time.

Where: Teachers pass out stickers and the students stick them on their chart outside of the classroom before they go home.

How: Every day at the end of the class, the teacher gives each student stickers related to the season. The teacher announces at the start of the day which behaviors will earn stickers. These can include paying attention during storytelling, turning in homework, and cleaning up after art work. The students who cooperate that day and display appropriate behaviors earn appropriate corresponding number of stickers—there is a daily maximum of three stickers.

STICKERS ON PAPER

Audience: Elementary.

Objective: To encourage positive behaviors and compliance with class rules.

Materials: Stickers, candy or small toys, and a copy of *sticker* paper.

Description: Students are rewarded to show immediate reinforcement for positive behavior, or for following classroom rules, or for completing tasks.

Use: Specific classroom implementation to be completed by the selecting teacher.

When: Use during class time.

Where: Use in the classroom.

How: The teacher explains that each student receives a copy of *sticker* paper that has an animal with 20 circles where the sticker goes. For each good behavior or completed task, each student receives a sticker that he or she places into one of the circles on the sheet. The filled circles (20 stickers all together) earn a healthy snack or a toy. Then, the student receives another sticker paper and can continue.

Suggestions: Ask the class to choose one kind of healthy snack that can be used throughout the year, such as sugarless Gummy Bears. This reward can be used in conjunction with the *Thumb Print* reward, for example, 20 stickers earn one thumb print (find *Thumb Print* below in this section).

STOPLIGHT

Audience: Lower elementary.

Objective: To encourage students to display appropriate behavior.

Materials: Large poster of a traffic stoplight, small pieces of paper (can be shaped like cars) with student's initials or names—one for each student. Around the green light are words describing what it means to be in the green (listening, hands on my own body, sitting crisscross applesauce (sitting cross-legged); around the yellow light are words to describe what it means to be in the yellow (interrupting, doodling, chewing gum); around the red light are words that describe what it means to be in the red (bolting, hitting, destroying property, spitting).

Description: At the beginning of each day, the students' cars are placed in the green light. Over the course of the day the car's position can change depending upon the student's behavior. Adults are responsible to monitor students' behavior and note where each student's car should be. Periodically during the day (after circle, math, before recess, before lunch) the stoplight is reviewed with the class to either remind students of where they are and what they can do to move their car back to green, or praise them for staying in the green.

Use: Specific classroom implementation to be completed by the selecting teacher.

When: Use every day.

Where: Use in the classroom, but the activity is to reflect the child's behavior in the entire school.

How: At the beginning of the year, the teacher presents the stoplight to the students and describes and role-plays activities that fit into each color. It is the job of the adults to move the students' cars to the appropriate color and to tell students why their cars are being moved. Preferred activities and rewards can be given to those students who, at the end of the day, remained on green the entire time.

Troubleshooting: The main problem with presenting the stoplight is that the behavior that is being discouraged is at the top and the behavior that is encouraged is at the bottom, simply because of the structure of a stoplight.

Note: Stoplight can be adapted to fit the context. It is excellent for small group work or stations.

SURPRISE MONEY

Audience: Upper elementary through high school.

Objective: To encourage classroom participation.

Materials: Play money (student made or bought).

Description: As students enter class and are seated, the teacher asks questions regarding the homework, yesterday's in-class discussion, or any other school topic. As students raise their hand and participate with answers, comments, or questions of their own, they get participation money. This money buys them their participation grade in the class.

Use: Specific classroom implementation to be completed by the selecting teacher.

When: At the beginning of class for review.

Where: The classroom.

How: At the beginning of the school year, the teacher establishes that class participation is important and valued. The teacher states that class participation heavily depends on the student's attendance; therefore, every student who is on time to class starts off with $5 for that day. To gain more money for their participation grade, the teacher then asks questions that review homework or previous class activities. Every question, comment, or answer contributed by a student will earn that student a dollar. This is a random process and is done on any given day that the teacher feels it is necessary. It needs to be clear to the students that money can be awarded at any time without previous warning. It is up to the teacher how to set the grade scale or to determine what the total amount of money possible is to receive a given participation grade. A student manager may help in the tallying and keeping track of monies.

Note: At the high school level, this system works well with ninth graders; however, it is not suggested for 10th through 12th grades. It also works very well for students in study skills classrooms, or other identified small groups of students who may be at risk for school failure.

TABLE OF THE WEEK

Audience: Elementary through junior high school.

Objective: To encourage positive and cooperative behavior in groups.

Materials: Large chart or space on board.

Description: Classroom management tool that enforces appropriate and cooperative behavior by individual students with the other students at their table. At the end of the school week, points are tallied to determine the table winner. Each group of students that wins receives various privileges, for example, free-time or a pizza party.

Use: Specific classroom implementation to be completed by the selecting teacher.

When: Best used when instructor is assigning group work during art, science, games, or language arts activities. However, when students are seated at group tables the instructor can reward the appropriate tables for being on-task, for being quiet, or for keeping their table neat.

Where: In the classroom where students are seated in groups. However, it can also be used in unstructured areas when students remind their group members to behave appropriately so that their group can receive the reward.

How: Seat students in groups—heterogeneously by tables. Establish and point out rules and standards of the school and classroom. After explaining consequences, introduce your expectations and reward system

    (1) tables receive tally points for behaving appropriately,

    (2) all students at a particular table group must participate in appropriate behavior,

    (3) if everyone at the table completes his or her work, he or she receives bonus points, and

    (4) the group that accumulates the most points becomes the *table of the week* for the following week.

Each group is allowed to choose several privileges. In addition, all groups receive rewards at the end of the week. Each group gets an opportunity to choose an activity to do during the last hour of the school week. The group with the most points chooses first, the group with the second most points chooses next, and so on. Rewards and privileges vary according to the grade level.

"TEACHER" DOLLARS

Audience: Upper elementary.

Objective: To encourage positive behavior in a thematic manner.

Material: Brightly colored paper with information on it about the *theme* of the unit being studied during thematic teaching units.

Description: *Dollars* worth extra credit are distributed to students who exhibit or characterize the *theme* of the unit being studied, that is generally a theme that teaches a social skill or another concept key to living cooperatively. The teacher names his or her dollars with their first or last names, for example, I call mine "Schultze" Dollars. For example, if Classical Greece is being studied, the theme of the unit might be *democracy*. The *dollars* illustrate examples of democracy or democratic ideals. So if the theme is Classical Greece, use a graphic of Pericles and the three goals he had for making Athens a better city. It is a good idea to have a mixture of *dollars* with slightly different aspects of the theme on them for variety and also to use as a teaching tool. Generally, the students love to read the information on the *dollars*.

Use: Specific classroom implementation to be completed by the selecting teacher.

When: Students are rewarded and given a *dollar* when they are observed exemplifying the *theme* being studied. They are not rewarded if they ask for the dollar. This is a good way to catch unaware students who are generally off-task and reward them for being on *theme*.

Where: At school, whenever the teacher or another adult observes the targeted theme being exemplified.

How: Teacher or other adults approach students either during whole-class, group, or individual instruction and compliment a student on behavior.

Example: The theme of Ancient China might be *respect*. The teacher attempts to "catch" a student who has difficulty respecting others in the act of being respectful. When this happens, the teacher immediately rewards the student with the *dollar* and compliments her or him on being so respectful and displaying an understanding of what the Chinese meant by *respect*.

Note: I especially like using these dollars as a way of rewarding students during small group instruction. I have used it successfully with groups who have on-task challenges or attention troubles by starting the lesson out by saying, "Everyone has already earned at least one dollar. I know that when we end the lesson everyone will get one, but let's review what we all need to do to earn it. Of course, it is possible that if you are not on task that means that you won't have earned your dollar, but that's not going to happen."

TEACHER'S SHOP

Audience: Lower elementary.

Objective: To encourage positive behavior in the classroom.

Materials: Fake money and special prizes.

Description: When a child follows directions and finishes work on time during the class time, the child is given a fake penny. At the end of the day, the child can exchange the pennies for fake coins or dollars of the same monetary value. At the end of the week, all students who have money can choose to buy any prize from the Teacher's Shop or save the money to use toward a better prize.

Use: Specific classroom implementation to be completed by the selecting teacher.

When: Throughout the school day.

Where: Anywhere at school.

How: At the beginning of the year the teacher establishes with the class what are considered rewarded behaviors. Rewarded behaviors can be defined as entering or exiting the class quietly, following class rules, finishing assignments on time, helping someone with a task, working quietly, and being on task. Whenever a child exemplifies rewarding behaviors, the child is given a fake penny. The penny may be given by the teacher or teaching assistant. At the end of each school day, from Monday through Thursday, the students can exchange pennies for a fake nickel, dime, quarter, or a dollar bill. On Friday, before the end of school, the class spends 5 minutes for the students to buy the prizes from the Teacher's Shop. The prizes can range from a pencil to an inexpensive gift certificate.

TEAM LEADERS

Audience: Elementary.

Objective: To encourage positive, cooperative, and self-management behaviors.

Materials: Some method of recording expected behavior, for example, placing bears in a jar, raising a thermometer, or filling a gumball machine. A visual chart that displays whose turn it is to be Team Leader and rules posted regarding expected behavior during a cooperative group activity time.

Descriptions: Cooperative groups are able to receive bears in a jar so that the entire class can obtain a goal. Each group has an assigned team leader who functions as a gatekeeper communicating expectations and encouraging students to stay focused.

Use: Specific classroom implementation to be completed by the selecting teacher.

When: During small cooperative group activity time.

Where: Within the classroom or anywhere that groups are needed.

How: First, brainstorm with the class the expected behavior of cooperative group work. The class seats should be arranged into groups of four to six students. There will a team leader assigned to each group. The team leader is responsible for reporting back to the teacher at the end of the period whether the group was following the rules of cooperative group work. The students should be focused on the positives taking place in the group and are not allowed to point out a student by name; this is not a *tattle* session. For each group that reports back positive, cooperative work a bear is placed in a jar. When the jar is full the class has reached their decided goal. For the thermometer, the teacher colors in a section so students can visually watch it rise. If you use gumballs, make sure the container is not too large so that students are unable to reach their goal.

The instructional goal is for students to be on task in cooperative groups and to tell the truth. Group-work products increase when students are given the responsibility of helping each other. Students will surprise you with their honesty about deserving the reward. The team leader should also be praised for their extra role of responsibility regardless of whether the group obtains the reward.

THANK YOU CARDS

Audience: Elementary through junior high school.

Objective: To encourage and acknowledge exceptional behavior.

Materials: Blank postcards or "Thank you" cards.

Description: When a student in class is putting forth extra effort or displaying exceptional behavior, gratitude, or courtesy, the teacher sends a personalized note, addressed to the student, thanking the student for the behavior.

Use: Specific classroom implementation to be completed by the selecting teacher.

When: The behavior(s) noticed during the course of the day are noted on a piece of paper. At the end of the day write a personalized thank you card to your student(s) acknowledging the behavior noticed that day.

Where: Use for any exceptional or out of the ordinary behavior.

How: On the same day the behavior occurs, you write a thank you card dated and addressed to the student written in your own handwriting. Be sure to specify the behavior exhibited by the student.

THERMOMETER

Audience: Elementary.

Objective: To encourage task completion and classwide positive behavior.

Materials: A large piece of paper with a drawing of a thermometer, and a marker pen.

Description: Students are rewarded for completing tasks and for good behavior. It is a class reward.

Use: Specific classroom implementation to be completed by the selecting teacher.

When: Use during class time.

Where: Use in the classroom.

How: At the beginning of the school year, the teacher posts a large piece of paper with the drawing of a thermometer on the bulletin board. The temperature will start at 0 degrees and increase up to 100 degrees. A red marker starts at the 0 degree mark. The teacher explains that as the students complete tasks as a group, such as book reports and homework on time, the mark will increase 5 degrees. This can also be used for attentive class behavior. When the class marker reaches 100 degrees, the teacher provides a surprise—anything fun works, such as a pizza party or a cookout at the teacher's house. The students can brainstorm the surprise at the beginning of the school year. This motivates the students to do their best.

THUMB PRINTS

Audience: Elementary.

Objective: To encourage positive behavior and task completion.

Materials: A large piece of white paper, ink pad, and markers.

Description: Students are rewarded for completing tasks and showing good behavior.

Use: Specific classroom implementation to be completed by the selecting teacher.

When: Use during class time.

Where: Use in the classroom.

How: At the beginning of the school year, the teacher puts a large piece of paper on the bulletin board that has a path going to a certain animal with a hidden surprise. There are about 10 animals along the path. The teacher explains that it takes about 30 to 50 thumb prints to reach each surprise. A completed task such as a book report, one chapter in math, and the weekly news earns a thumb print. A student presses her or his thumb on the ink pad and then presses it on the path on the white paper. The student puts their initials on the thumb print and then can draw an animal shape or another shape from it. Exhibiting good behavior when the teacher is absent and a substitute teacher fills in, being helpful toward others, or whatever the teacher is impressed by earns a thumb print. When the thumb prints reach the drawing of the animal, the teacher opens up the surprise to see what the reward is for the class. The reward can be a pizza party, another type of party, or an in-class movie with popcorn. Remember the teacher has the freedom to determine which tasks or good behavior earns a thumb print for each student. This encourages the students to do their best.

Suggestions: The path can be drawn creatively in the shape of a schoolhouse or a yellow brick road to Oz.

TICKETS

Audience: Elementary.

Objective: To encourage appropriate and on-task behavior.

Materials: A roll of prize tickets or photocopy tickets of a similar size.

Description: When a child is following the procedures for the activity in a timely and complete manner, the teacher gives her or him a ticket with the child's name or initials on the back in the teacher's handwriting.

Use: Specific classroom implementation to be completed by the selecting teacher.

When: During independent work time, arts, or structured play time.

Where: In the classroom.

How: At the beginning of the year, the teacher describes the behavior that is expected. He or she explains that from time to time *tickets* will be given out when students are demonstrating expected classroom behavior. The teacher may act out or set up a role-play to model the behaviors considered appropriate. A chart on the wall shows what the teacher and class have decided is the "way we do things in this class" and provides a constant reminder of the expected behaviors. The teacher tells the students that tickets will not be given out in every work time, but that if they are working according to the class rules, they will get tickets some of the time. The teacher needs to be very sure that all students get this reward some of the time and that no one group of students is favored. This requires careful self-monitoring on the part of the teacher and is beneficial for that reason as well. During work times as the teacher is circulating throughout the room, tickets are given to students who are working appropriately.

After a predetermined amount of time (generally a week or more), the students can turn in a certain number of tickets for a reward. These rewards include requesting a preferred song for the class to sing, or free art time, computer time, media center privileges, and the like. Sometimes you can give students a turn at the grab bag (with goodies in it) or take them out for a snack.

I have noticed that students adapt very well to the intermittent nature of the reward provided it is explained as just that: some of the people, some of the time. Many get in the work habit in hopes of the reward and the habit sticks even when the reward is not immediate.

UNIT LOG/"TABLE OF CONTENTS"

Audience: Upper elementary.

Objective: To teach organizational skills.

Materials: One or two sheets of blank Unit Log/"Table of Contents" sheets.

Description: These are generic unit logs/table of contents pages tailored by the teacher to fit units being studied. They are meant as an alternative way for students to teach themselves organizational skills through the use of a table of contents.

Use: Specific classroom implementation to be completed by the selecting teacher.

When: Designed for organization and introduced at the beginning of a new unit in social studies, science or any topic that has a separate folder, or section.

Where: In the classroom, during academic instruction.

How: The Unit Log/Table of Contents is introduced to the whole class at the beginning of a teaching unit.

Example:

Name: _____   Date: _____

TABLE OF CONTENTS: CLASSICAL GREECE

Assignment

_____   _____   _____

_____   _____   _____

The class is told that they may find it useful to have a Unit Log/Table of Contents in their unit folder. Teacher and class go over briefly what a table of contents is and then the teacher gives an example for how the children use a table of contents. The dialogue might be,

"If I were using it, I would write down the date work was assigned, the name of the assignment, and then I would use the other two columns for *date due* and for *checking off* when I finished the assignment."

By using the unit log/table of contents it makes finding their assignments easier, they are better organized, and quite probably this can lead to a better grade on the unit. The teacher models by having a facsimile Unit Log/Table of Contents posted on chart paper that is updated as assignments are made.

VIP PASSES

Audience: Upper elementary through junior high school.

Objective: To encourage students to be prepared for class.

Materials: Passes.

Description: Students receive one VIP Pass each time they are in class, seated, and ready to work when the bell rings.

Use: Specific classroom implementation to be completed by the selecting teacher.

When: Every day.

Where: In the classroom.

How: To encourage being in class on time, a Pass Manager is designated to issue passes to each student who meets the on-time criteria. These passes accumulate during the week and can be traded in on Friday of each week. The pass manager handles the trades as follows:

1 pass = 5 minutes in-class free time;

2 passes = a food pass;

10 passes = a worthy designated activity or the ability to apply for the Pass Manager position.

The student can save passes to trade for more free time on academically fun activities, such as computer time.

WALL MAP

Audience: Upper elementary.

Objective: To encourage cooperative behavior.

Materials: Wall map (can be made by students themselves), sticky dots in various colors designated for each team of four. Schedule a party for the group as a reward at a predetermined time. Ice cream, pizza, video, and popcorn are a few suggested rewards.

Description: Groups are picked with the teacher's help (making sure students with varying abilities are together) to work cooperatively to earn travel dots for their total scores on spelling, dictation, and journal work. The group with the highest points wins a party during school. This can happen monthly, or after each unit. Bonus dots can be earned at the discretion of the teacher for conduct, attitude, etc. This allows students at every level to *win* when working together as a team fostering positive peer interaction.

Use: Specific classroom implementation to be completed by the selecting teacher.

When: From the beginning of the semester. Designate length (4 weeks, 6 weeks, 9 weeks).

Where: In the classroom setting.

How: At the beginning of the semester, each group cooperatively chooses a group name and a destination (for example, castle, galaxy, fort, fantasy land) and makes a coordinating game piece (usually made out of cardboard). These destinations are drawn on a classroom map (large, white butcher paper on bulletin board) by each group with an appropriate number of dots leading to them (i.e., if there are 10 tests at 5 dots each = 50 dots). Groups earn dots by getting the most points for any given quiz, test, or journal assignment and are able to move their game piece accordingly. The first group to get to their destination wins. By having many games and changing group configurations during the semester, all students can experience success.

WATCH ME GROW

Audience: Elementary.

Objective: To encourage students to take pride in their work.

Materials: Student folders (or portfolios) with a certain type of work (math practice, writing).

Description: At the end of selected lessons or activities, collect and evaluate papers and place them in the student's folders. Do this for several months, always choosing a product that builds or expands on a skill that is collected in the student's special folder.

Use: Specific classroom implementation to be completed by the selecting teacher.

When: Start close to the beginning of the year and continue through until the last few weeks of school.

Where: In the classroom.

How: During one or more class sessions (where the teacher does not need to monitor the accuracy or student work) pull one folder at a time and show the student his or her progress as demonstrated by the work in the folder.

This does require teacher involvement, but when the students can visually track and recognize their growth they are intrinsically rewarded with a greater sense of accomplishment, progress, and recognition. At a free time, the teacher may even allow them to pull their own folders, look at what is inside, and give themselves a pat on the back. Students can show their folders at Back to School Night and Open House.

When the folders become too full, ask the student to choose work that is no longer needed and have them take it home. If the student has trouble deciding, use one of the student–teacher conferences to help in the process.

WEEKLY GRID

Audience: Upper elementary through junior high school.

Objective: To encourage self-management of time and behavior.

Materials: A grid form (pre-made Excel Chart, Microsoft Word table) that allows the student to fill in the following information: assignments for the upcoming week and the due dates, a goal for the week, and comments by the student and teacher.

Description: The grid is an instrument used by the students to plan their week, laying out the due dates in an organized, standard fashion. Along with this, the students also use a long-range calendar that they take the information from to concentrate on the individual week. The main objective of the weekly grid is to give students a tool to establish a goal for the week and then evaluate their own performance for the week. The intrinsic reward comes from the students' own evaluation of their work. Watching this activity progress over a year, it is obvious that the students get the most satisfaction out of reaching their goals. Comments range from: "My goal was to improve my math score from a *C* to a *B*, but I got a 90 percent. I am very happy with my work." "My goal was to stay away from Matt during recess this week, because he says things to me I do not like. I only saw him once, and he did not say anything to me. I accomplished my goal for the week."

Use: Specific classroom implementation to be completed by the selecting teacher.

When: Daily.

Where: In the classroom.

How: The grid is used on a daily basis. On Monday, the students write down the assignments for the week and establish their goals for the week. Throughout the week as assignments are turned in, the teacher checks off the work on the top part of the grid for each student. On Friday the student evaluates his or her work performance, writes comments, and discusses if their goal was reached or not. The teacher examines the grid daily. This can be somewhat labor intensive but it gives the teacher a chance to interact with the students one on one for a few minutes each day. The teacher can set up a portion of the language/arts period each day as an independent work period where students work on a prescribed task such as writing on their essay thus allowing time for the teacher to discuss other student's weekly grids. The teacher uses this time to confer with the students on an individual basis.

WITHOUT A RAFFLE

Audience: Elementary.

Objective: To encourage on-task behavior.

Description: This is an individual contingency reward system. Students are given tickets for good behavior and then have the opportunity to use those tickets to *buy* prizes such as pencils, notebooks, and toys.

Materials: Raffle tickets, or stamped cards, inexpensive prizes such as little toys, and recycled or used items of good quality.

Use: Specific classroom implementation to be completed by the selecting teacher.

When: During class time especially transition times.

Where: In the classroom.

How: Use during transitions in the classroom to reward those who follow directions and who immediately come in quietly from recess, ready to work. Tickets are handed out to these students as the teacher walks around to observe. At the end of each week, the student store is open and students can buy items if they have enough tickets. The items vary in how many tickets they cost. Students can save their tickets to get a higher-priced item at a later date.

YELLOW/BLUE SHEET REWARDS

Audience: Elementary through junior high school.

Objective: To encourage homework completion.

Materials: Half sheets of yellow and blue copy paper and prizes.

Description: When a student completes all of his or her homework for the week, he or she receives a yellow sheet indicating the accomplishment of homework completion. The students who did not complete all of their homework assignments for the week get a blue sheet reminding them of what they need to work on during the weekend and to return to school by Monday morning. When students receive a certain number of yellow sheets they can turn them in for a prize. Even students who earn a blue sheet can turn them in for a prize because two blues that have been cleared (the missing work has been completed and handed in on time) equal one yellow. This is a great way of helping students build responsibility for completing homework assignments.

Use: Specific classroom implementation to be completed by the selecting teacher.

When: Throughout the school year. Sheets are given out on Friday.

Where: In the classroom.

How: On the yellow sheets print out a saying congratulating the students for being responsible and for completing all of their homework assignments for the week. On the blue sheets print out a saying reminding the students that completing homework is part of learning responsibility and leave a space so you can list the homework assignments that are missing and that they will need to complete over the weekend and turn in Monday. Have a reward chart posted in the room so students know what rewards or prizes they can receive for their yellow and blue sheets.

Examples:

Number of yellows	Reward
5 sheets	Free pencil, eraser, paper
10 sheets	Free homework pass
15 sheets	Free coke, ice cream
25 sheets	Free lunch

You can change the number and rewards to best fit your students.

Closing Remarks

eachers must find a classroom management system that works for them and is easy to implement, or they will spend more time managing behavior and less time on instruction. Creating rapport with students emanates from a clear classroom structure where students understand their limits. The best teachers know that building trust and good relationships with their students requires clear expectations of behavior, a mix of appropriate positive and negative consequences, and a belief that children want to do their best and have a desire to learn. It must be stressed over and over that a classroom management system has to be part of a positive learning environment, wherein students feel encouraged to achieve, connected to one another, and value their learning. If those elements are not present, the classroom management system will have the opposite effect and achievement will be compromised.

For most students a "yellow light" always goes off before a "red light"; they will always send a smoke signal out before their behavior escalates into a brush fire. So it is incumbent upon the teacher to anticipate the potential for misbehavior and then remove what may be causing it—*Be Proactive*. For example, if a student is shoving other students in the middle of a line then the teacher removes the child from the line and places the child at the back of the line and then keeps close tabs on the student. By anticipating potential behavioral problems teachers avert behavior from escalating, therefore eliminating the need for imposing oftentimes harsh penalties for fairly benign misbehavior.

Attuned teachers develop positive relationships with their students which builds a true sense of the student as a stakeholder in the community of the classroom. They allow students to help establish classroom behavioral expectations, provide multiple opportunities for students to interact and solve problems, and clearly understand the importance of creating an ethical, moral, and caring environment so students can truly take responsibility for their actions and feelings.

Of course, children with intense behavior needs should be provided with a more involved prescriptive behavior method; these children benefit from a method that is individualized with an identified plan of action. Special educators are adept at helping general educators devise positive behavior support plans for children with more intense behavioral challenges.

I sincerely hope that you discover the value of this resource and that you find teaching as enjoyable as I have found it to be over the years. Remember to always keep a sense of humor—it makes managing a classroom less a burden and more of a joy.

GET YOUR ACTIVITY PUBLISHED

I trust that you will find the activities in the book to be of interest. As mentioned, these are but a few good ideas that teachers use in their classrooms to help students grow socially and emotionally. Now it is your turn to share an activity to encourage positive student behavior with teachers nationwide. The guidelines are simple:

- Use *only* the template on the next page and fill in all the fields (use one of the examples from this book as a guide).
- Make sure your activity fits on one or two pages-spacing 1½ not single or double-spaced. Use Microsoft Word to publish your activity.
- Write your activity in a clear, concrete, and concise manner so that teachers can understand and immediately use in their classrooms.
- Make sure that the grammar is correct and check for typos.
- Email your activity as an attachment directly to Dr. Lou Denti at ldenti@csumb.edu.

Make certain to include your contact information when you send it by mail or electronically.

Contact information: Name:
    Home or school address:
    E-mail address:

If you are adapting an activity from another source or teacher make certain to give appropriate credit and include contact information as well.
Thank you and I look forward to seeing your activity in print.

ACTIVITY TEMPLATE

(Name of Activity)

Audience:

Objective:

Materials:

Description:

Use:

When:

Where:

How:

Source:

Resources

WEBSITE RESOURCES

Barkley, R. (2005). *ADHD and the nature of self-control.* Retrieved from http://www.russellbarkley.org/adhd-facts.htm.

Children and Adults with Attention-Deficit/Hyperactivity Disorder (CHADD). (2011). *CHADD live.* Retrieved from http://www.chadd.org/?gclid=CNb-oJnC1pwCFR4HagodZ17QwA.

Curriculum Associates. (n.d.). *Skills/advanced skills for school success: Grades 3–7+.* Retrieved from http://www.curriculumassociates.com/products/detail.asp?title=SkillsSS.

Devereux Center. (2003–2011). Retrieved from http://www.devereux.org.

Ellerd, D., Harrower, J., & Powell, D. (2011). *Framework of support for students with special needs: Supporting positive behavior.* Retrieved from http://teachingcommons.cdl.edu/education/learners/supporting_positive_behav.html.

Jones, F. (2001). *Tools for Teaching.* Retrieved from http://www.fredjones.com.

Kansas Institute for Positive Behavior Support. (2011). Retrieved from http://www.kipbs.org/new_kipbs/index/html.

LD Online. (2008). *Behavior and social skills.* Retrieved from http://www.ldonline.org/questions/behavior.

Levine, M. (2008). Message from Dr. Mel Levine. In *Learning Disabilities Resource.* Retrieved from http://www.success-in-mind.org.

Namka, L. (1996–2010). Bully behavior lesson plans. In *Talk, Trust and Feel, Therapeutics.* Retrieved from http://www.angriesout.com/bullylessons.html.

National School Forms, Inc. (1965–2011). A complete line of educational forms serving discipline, progress, administrative, and transportation needs. Retrieved from http://www.SchoolForms.com.

Pearson Education Development. (2000–2008). *Laying the foundation for positive classroom behavior.* Retrieved from http://www.teachervision.fen .com/classroom-management/teaching-methods/6400.html.

Teachers touch hearts. (2011) *The behavior management page.* [Electronic message board]. http://www.teachingheart.net/classroombehaviormanage.html.

Tobin, T. (2011). *PBIS, Positive behavioral intervention & supports.* [University of Oregon presentation and resource list]. Retrieved from http://www.uoregon .edu/~ttobin.

Wong, H., & Wong, R. (2011). Effective Teaching. *Teachers Net Gazette 8,* (9). Retrieved from http://teachers.net/gazette/wong.html.

Wright's Law Behavior Problems and Discipline. Retrieved from http:// www.wrightslaw.com.

BIBLIOGRAPHY

Archer, A., & Gleason, M. (n.d.). *Skills for school success series (Grades 3–6).* North Billerica, MA: Curriculum Associates.

This research-based program transforms "strategy-free" students into successful students who exhibit positive classroom behaviors: manage time, organize assignments, make effective use of texts and reference books, interpret graphic aids, gather information, take notes, respond in class, and study for and approach tests with confidence.

Archer, A., & Hughes, C. (2010). *Explicit instruction: Effective and efficient teaching.* New York, NY: Guilford Press.

This new book is a masterful work of art showing how to instruct diverse learners in modern-day classrooms. The book guides the teacher through the most important components of effective instruction with cogent examples and strategies.

Barell, J. (2003). *Developing more curious minds.* Alexandria, VA: Association for Supervision and Curriculum Development.

This book encourages teachers to instill in students the need to search for answers by examining their own process of learning about things that interest them. Whether a teacher uses lessons that provide guided inquiry or allows students a more open-ended approach to exploration, the ultimate goal is to prepare students to become self-reliant and independent thinkers. By following what puzzles and/or interests them, students find their own natural motivation for learning.

Barell, J. (2007). *Problem-based learning: An inquiry approach* (2nd ed.). Thousand Oaks, CA: Corwin.

> This book helps teachers create environments wherein they and their students can work with complex, intriguing situations that foster inquiry, research, and the deriving of reasonable conclusions.

Benson, H. (1975). *The relaxation response.* New York, NY: HarperCollins.

> The Relaxation Response is a simple practice that once learned takes 10 to 20 minutes a day and can help relieve stress and tension. This best-selling book written by a medical doctor helps one improve one's mental, physical and emotional health. It's easy for teachers to thumb through the book with a new updated forward by Dr. Benson.

Branden, N. (1999). *The art of living consciously: The power of awareness to transform everyday life.* New York, NY: Fireside.

> This book is an excellent resource on how to promote and maintain self-esteem. Branden challenges the reader in all of his works to consider the importance of maintaining emotional balance and provides insights and ideas on how to do so (available through http://www.amazon.com).

Canter, L. (2009). *Assertive discipline: Positive behavior management for today's classroom* (4th ed.). Bloomington, IN: Solution Tree.

> Up-to-date strategies that address the complex issue of managing student behavior in the classroom. For K–12 teachers (available on Amazon.com).

Fisher, R., & Ury, W. (1991). *Getting to yes: Negotiating agreement without giving in* (2nd ed.). New York, NY: Penguin Books.

> *Getting to Yes: Negotiating Agreement Without Giving In* is a very practical book on how to negotiate and resolve conflicts. For teachers, the book is extremely helpful when negotiation is mandated with students, parents, administrators, or colleagues; this book dictates a very positive and rewarding approach.

Glasser, W. (1998). *Choice theory: A new psychology of personal freedom.* New York, NY: HarperCollins.

> *Choice Theory* by William Glasser is a must read for educators. Dr. Glasser lays out his theory of internal motivation in a practical and eloquent manner that is easy to digest. He strongly believes in an individual's ability to choose. He makes a convincing argument that we all have more control over our behaviors than people might think and that we are responsible for the choices we make.

Glenn, H. S., & Nelsen, J. (2000). *Raising self-reliant children in a self-indulgent world: Seven building blocks for developing capable young people* (Revised ed.). Roseville, CA: Prima.

Stephen Glenn has a knack for making difficult concepts easy to understand and put into practice for both parents and teachers. This book is a good read. Teachers can use the seven building blocks as a way to build a strong foundation for students learning how to be more responsible, caring, and capable.

Johns, B. H., & Carr, V. G. (1995). *Techniques for managing verbally and physically aggressive students.* Columbia, MO: Hawthorne Educational Services.

This book provides clear guidelines on how to de-escalate aggressive behavior. Johns and Carr write in a very easy to understand manner giving teachers practical steps to deal with students who for one reason or another are verbally and physically aggressive.

Johnson, D., Johnson, R., Holubec, E. J. (1991). *Cooperation in the classroom.* Edina, MN: Interaction Book.

This book is one of the finest resources on cooperative learning theory and how it impacts students in public school classrooms. Reading about cooperative learning theory from the researchers who developed the theory gives educators the essential background knowledge needed for implementation.

Jones, F. (2007). *Tools for teaching: Discipline, instruction, and motivation* (2nd ed.). Santa Cruz, CA: Fred Jones.

In *Tools for Teaching*, Dr. Jones describes the skills by which exceptional teachers make the classroom a place of success and enjoyment for both themselves and their students. *Tools for Teaching* integrates the management of discipline, instruction, and motivation into a system that allows you to reduce the stress of teaching by preventing most management headaches.

Kagan, S., & Kagan, M. (2011). *Kagan cooperative learning.* San Clemente, CA: Kagan.

Here is what Spencer and Miguel write about their new book. "The book that started it all—is all NEW! Why would the Kagans completely revise and revamp a classic that has sold nearly half a million copies? The answer: So much has changed! Cooperative Learning today is different. This new book presents today's most successful cooperative learning methods. The Kagans make it easier than ever to boost engagement and achievement. You'll still find all the practical and proven Kagan Structures, including Numbered Heads Together, Round Table, and Three-Step Interview—direct from the man who invented cooperative learning structures. And there's still plenty of ready-to-do teambuilding and class building activities to make your class click." Spencer Kagan is so practical. Be sure to pick up this resource and check out his website at http://www.kaganonline.com.

Marzano, R. J., Pickering, D., & Pollack, J. E. (2001). *Classroom instruction that works: Research-based strategies for increasing student achievement.* Alexandria, VA: Association for Supervision and Curriculum Development.

For any educator who hungers after real proof of which teaching strategies raise student achievement and by how much, this K–12 guide provides a banquet of research evidence, statistical data, and case studies. Distilling decades of information into a clear plan of action, the authors identify nine categories of instructional strategies that maximize student learning and explain the vital details you need to know about each.

Nelsen, J. (2006). *Positive discipline.* New York, NY: Random House.

The key to discipline is not punishment, but mutual respect. All parents try to do their best—but the best of intentions doesn't always produce the best results. Dr. Jane Nelsen, an experienced psychologist, educator, and mother believes that children misbehave when they feel thwarted in their need to belong and in their need for love and attention. Dr. Nelson is best known for her parenting books; however, she has created a wonderful series of her timeworn tips for teachers, preschool through adolescents (Jane Nelson's books are available on Amazon. com).

Sprague, J., & Golly, A. (2004). *Best behavior: Building positive behavior support in schools.* Frederick, CO: Sopris West.

This book helps teachers develop a comprehensive schoolwide behavioral approach to meet the needs of all learners. Specific and detailed strategies for managing the classroom are provided, as well as how to work with students with behavioral challenges. Dr. Sprague's positive behavior support model allows educators to tailor their behavioral plans and approaches to meet the needs of students. This is an excellent resource for administrators who are searching for a tool to guide schoolwide reform (available through Barnes and Noble).

Thompson, R. (personal communication, 2011). *Daily class procedures.* In elementary special education syllabus, Gilroy Unified School District, Gilroy, California.

Mr. Thompson teaches students with moderate to severe disabilities. He developed his Daily Class Procedures to systemize operating procedures in the class. Since the students need reminders and repetition, he reviews the procedures daily and consistently rewards students for following outlined procedures.

U. S. Department of Education, The National Institute of Education. [ca. 1980]. *Reducing behavior problems in the elementary school classroom: Five ways to manage a classroom.* Washington, DC: Government Printing Office.

The National Institute of Education (NIE) was abolished and subsumed under the name OERI, Office of Educational Research and Improvement, in 1985. This book was produced by the U.S. Department of Education to be copied and used by teachers. These five ways have been a mainstay in my inservice programs with teachers. I draw on them in my book to help teachers realize that adopting a few essential tips on how to manage your classroom is critical to achieving success throughout one's career.

Walker, H. M., Ramsey, E., & Gresham, F. M. (2003). *Antisocial behavior in schools: Evidence-based practices* (2nd ed.). Florence, KY: Cengage Learning.

This text is intended to provide educators with increased understanding of the nature, origins, and causes of antisocial behavior and to offer information on the best available practices, interventions, and model programs for preventing and remediating antisocial behavior disorders occurring in school (available through Barnes and Noble.com).

Wiggins, G., & McTighe, J. (2005). *Understanding by design* (Expanded 2nd ed.). Alexandria, VA: Association for Supervision and Curriculum Development.

All teachers work toward designing a classroom that truly maximizes the potential of learners. In this book Wiggins and McTighe help teachers design learning experiences that make it much more likely that students understand content and apply it in meaningful ways.

Wong, H. K., & Wong, R. (2009). *The first days of school: How to be an effective teacher.* Mountain View, CA: Harry K.Wong.

This book provides a clear, step-by-step approach for organizing one's classroom. It is a very helpful and practical resource for all teachers.

E + R = C WALL POSTER

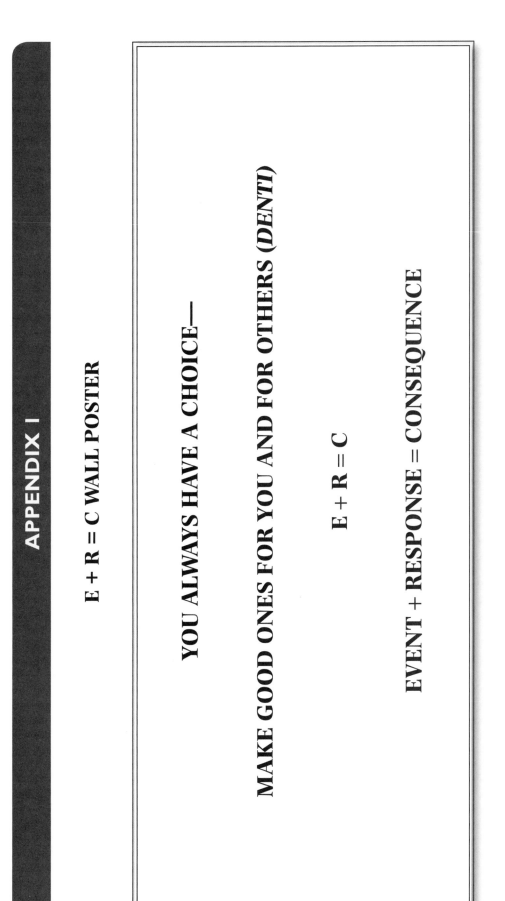

YOU ALWAYS HAVE A CHOICE—

MAKE GOOD ONES FOR YOU AND FOR OTHERS (*DENTI*)

E + R = C

EVENT + RESPONSE = CONSEQUENCE

IeAM CAPABLE WALL POSTER

Identify and use a method that is easy to implement

establish clear limits and follow through

Apply appropriate consequences immediately!

Maintain a consistent approach to foster trust and respect

IeAM SYSTEM TEMPLATE

(Identify) MY CLASSROOM MANAGEMENT APPROACH

(establish) GROUND RULES FOR MY MANAGEMENT APPROACH

(Apply) APPROPRIATE CONSEQUENCES

(Maintain) CONSISTENCY

APPENDIX 4

CHECKING MYSELF BOXES

CHECKING MYSELF BOX

Checklist Item:

Rating:

Checklist Question:

Response and Action:

APPENDIX 5

MY PROGRESS GOALS

Once a student has completed the school behavior checklist by himself or herself or with the teacher's assistance, chose one of the items from the lists titled *Before School Class Behavior*, *During School Class Behavior* or *After School Class Behavior*, and that you rated as *Partially Mastered* or *Needs Help With*. Discuss the items with your teacher, write your goals down, and begin working on them right away. At the end of the first or second week, indicate whether you accomplished the goal by circling *Yes* or by circling *In Progress* meaning that the goal is still unfinished. A *My Progress Goals* folder should be created and kept in the classroom for students to complete and to use to develop and record new goals. The teacher may want to schedule a time for this activity. Students could share their goals with a partner or in a small group to receive feedback. The *My Progress Goals* activity promotes students taking responsibility for their behavior and getting support for working toward their identified goals from other students and/or from their teacher.

Goals:

BEFORE:

First Week: Yes   In Progress

Second Week: Yes   In Progress

WHEN IN CLASS:

First Week: Yes   In Progress

Second Week: Yes   In Progress

AFTER/AT HOME:

First Week: Yes   In Progress

Second Week: Yes   In Progress

APPENDIX 6

CONFLICT RESOLUTION FORM

Conflict Resolution Coordinator(s) _____

Date _____

Who had the conflict? _____

What kind of conflict?

      ❑ Argument   ❑ Fight   ❑ Rumor   ❑ Other

How did you find out about it?

      ❑ Student   ❑ Yard Duty Supervisor   ❑ Teacher
      ❑ Aide   ❑ Counselor   ❑ Yourself

What was the conflict about? _____

Was the conflict resolved? _____ Yes _____ No

Resolution:

Student #1 agrees to	Student # 2 agrees to

APPENDIX 7

SCATTERPLOT—DATA RECORDING FORM

Student:		Target behavior:
Observer:		
Start date:		
End date:		

Using a scatter plot involves recording the times of the day (and/or activities) in which the behavior does and does not occur to identify patterns that occur over days and/or weeks.

	Dates										
Time	Activity										
Behavior did not occur											
Behavior occurred											
NA Not observed											

174

APPENDIX 8

DISCIPLINARY REFERRAL

STUDENT'S NAME	DATE OF INCIDENT
CLASS	PERIOD-TIME OF DAY
TEACHER	

NOTICE TO PARENTS

1. The purpose of this notice is to inform you to a disciplinary incident involving the student.
2. Please note the action taken by the teacher and the corrective action initiated today.

REASON(S) FOR THIS NOTICE:

- ☐ CUTTING CLASS
- ☐ EXCESSIVE TARDINESS
- ☐ LEFT GROUNDS WITHOUT PERMISSION
- ☐ ANNOYING TO CLASSMATES
- ☐ DESTRUCTIVE TO SCHOOL
- ☐ LITTERING
- ☐ RUDE/DISCOURTEOUS
- ☐ EXCESSIVE TALKING
- ☐ UNACCEPTABLE LANGUAGE
- ☐ FIGHTING
- ☐ DISRUPTIVE/UNCOOPERATIVE
- ☐ _____

ACTION TAKEN PRIOR TO THIS NOTICE:

- ☐ REVIEWED STUDENT'S FILE
- ☐ HAD CONFERENCE WITH STUDENT
- ☐ CONSULTED COUNSELOR
- ☐ CHANGED STUDENT'S SEAT
- ☐ DETAINED STUDENT AFTER SCHOOL
- ☐ TELEPHONED PARENT
- ☐ HAD CONFERENCE WITH PARENT
- ☐ SENT PREVIOUS NOTICE(S)
- ☐ _____

PRESENT ACTION AND RECOMMENDATION(S):

- ☐ STUDENTS REPRIMANDED
- ☐ PARENT CONFERENCE RECOMMENDED
- ☐ STUDENT WILL MAKE UP TIME
- ☐ STUDENT PLACED ON PROBATION
- ☐ STUDENT SUSPENDED
- ☐ MATTER REFERRED TO:
- ☐ _____

_____ _____

(Action Taken By)   (Date)

Form #55–National School Forms, Inc.

PINK-PARENTS' COPY   GREEN-OFFICE COPY   GOLD-TEACHER'S COPY

National School Forms, Inc. (www.SchoolForms.com) Complete line of educational forms serving Discipline, Progress, Administrative, and Transportation needs. Family owned and operated since 1965. 1-800-431-1201.

Index

CORWIN

A SAGE Company

The Corwin logo—a raven striding across an open book—represents the union of courage and learning. Corwin is committed to improving education for all learners by publishing books and other professional development resources for those serving the field of PreK–12 education. By providing practical, hands-on materials, Corwin continues to carry out the promise of its motto: **"Helping Educators Do Their Work Better."**